Alma Will is an immigrant who has called the UK home for over 20 years. At 43, she has emerged from years of an unfulfilling life and being in toxic relationships, grappling with unhealthy behaviours that once led her to despair and hopelessness. In her darkest moments, she turned to God for forgiveness and strength, seeking the courage to restart her life after 40. Through perseverance and faith, she reclaimed her independence and freedom—dreams she once believed were lost.

Though Alma never considered herself a writer, she discovered a passion for storytelling during her journey of self-discovery. Journaling became a powerful outlet for her emotions and experiences, allowing her to process her thoughts and reflect on her life.

This newfound love for writing not only facilitated Alma's healing but also illuminated the complexities of her past choices. As an advocate for mental health and well-being, Alma hopes this book inspires other women to embrace change, confront the challenges in their lives, and pursue true happiness.

Alma believes life is magical, and that magic lies within each of us. We must find the courage to choose change and maintain faith in the journey, just as she has.

Alma has come to recognise that it is never too late to understand how the people in our lives can influence our paths—some may lead us into darkness, while others guide us towards the light. Ultimately, the power to choose your path is always in your hands. If she can overcome her challenges, so can you. Find your faith, ask, open your heart and be ready to receive the blessings life has to offer.

Each day is a precious gift, an opportunity to start anew. Let us cherish the chance to wake up every morning and make the most of it—because life is beautiful, and so are you.

I dedicate this book to two extraordinary individuals who helped me emerge from the darkness that once enveloped my mind.

To my therapist, Angie: thank you for standing by my side, listening to my struggles, and witnessing my tears. I apologise for the times I said I was okay when I wasn't and for the mask I wore while everything around me seemed to sink. Even when the voices in my head were disturbing me, your unwavering support and belief in my strength illuminated a path towards healing.

And to you, who unknowingly mended my broken heart and nurtured my lost soul: I am eternally grateful for you. Thank you for holding my hand through the tough times, for showing me the light, and for helping me rediscover joy and playfulness within myself. My love for you has transformed my life in ways I never imagined, and I hope I have brought a fraction of that light to yours.

Alma Will

Darkness to Light: The Love that Saved Her

Austin Macauley Publishers®
London * Cambridge * New York * Sharjah

The story, experiences, and words are the author's alone.

A CIP catalogue record for this title is available from the British Library.

ISBN 9781035897445 (Paperback)
ISBN 9781035897452 (Hardback)
ISBN 9781035897469 (ePub e-book)

www.austinmacauley.com

First Published 2025
Austin Macauley Publishers Ltd®
1 Canada Square
Canary Wharf
London
E14 5AA

I thank God for His unwavering guidance, love and strength throughout this journey. It is through His grace that I found the courage to transform my life and share this story. Without His inspiration, this book would not have been possible.

I am deeply grateful for the personal development tools that have guided me, especially the timeless wisdom of stoicism. The teachings of philosophers like Marcus Aurelius and Seneca have been instrumental in shaping my understanding of resilience, self-reflection, and growth. Their wisdom has been a steady companion, helping me navigate life's challenges with love and clarity.

I also acknowledge the power of love, both divine and human – which has been the driving force behind my healing and transformation. It is love that opens hearts, enabling me to believe in myself and in the possibility of a brighter future.

This book is a reflection of my faith, my personal growth, and the lessons I've learned along the way. To anyone seeking their own path to healing and transformation, I hope this story serves as a reminder that change is possible, and that love whether from God or others has the power to light our way.

Chapter 1
Yearning for Change

Everything began on Thursday, the 27th of June. My morning started like any other: coffee warming my hands as I stood by the window, gazing at the grey London sky, longing for a change so powerful it would ripple through every part of my life. I craved transformation—personal, professional, mental, and spiritual. As I watched the clouds drift slowly across the muted sky, I felt the ache of their freedom, a stark contrast to the weight pressing down on me. And in that stillness, I came face-to-face with a hard truth: I was deeply dissatisfied with who I had become.

My professional life was in disarray, tangled in a career change that left me lost in confusion and doubt. My personal life, too, had fractured; I'd recently walked away from a long, draining relationship that seemed to sap my spirit, offering neither joy nor the fulfilment I so desperately needed. Each day felt like a struggle, and somewhere inside, I yearned to rediscover myself. I felt as though I'd buried my true self beneath layers of neglect, putting aside my own dreams until I no longer recognised who I was. I had become distant, a shadow of the person I'd once hoped to be, weighed down by unmet expectations and deferred dreams. And in the quietest, heaviest moments, I found myself wishing I could just slip away, escaping to a place where the ache of reality could no longer touch me.

But that day, without knowing it, I was on the cusp of something unavoidable.

There I sat, alone in my small Hampstead studio, gazing out the wide window framing a row of neighbouring flats. The walls around me were painted a stark white, meant to calm, but instead, the silence pressed on me, echoing with thoughts I'd tried to ignore. The stillness amplified every regret, every self-doubt, and every hour I'd let slip by, making the silence feel almost oppressive.

For so long, I'd poured myself into others, letting their needs overshadow my own. The relationship I had just left had deepened that habit, suffocating the spark of who I was and leaving me to drift in a life that felt smaller and darker each day. Looking back, I see now that I wasn't simply avoiding my own issues; I was running from the vibrant person I could have been, caught in a cycle that left me feeling more alone than ever.

Yet that morning, a glimmer of hope lingered, fragile but present. Later that afternoon, I would meet an old friend—a steady presence in my life for the past five years, someone who had always seemed to know when I needed a break from my own mind. I often called him my "psychiatrist," though he was far from a professional. He was simply a friend with whom I could talk about anything and everything. With him, I could forget my worries, losing myself in laughter, easy conversation, and the kind of warmth that made the world feel lighter. He had a gift for listening, seeming to see past my walls and helping me remember that I could still laugh, still feel joy, even if only for a while.

Unbeknownst to me, that afternoon would be the first step on a journey I'd needed far more than I knew.

I meticulously organised my flat to make the afternoon special. The scent of freshly baked cookies wafted through the air, adding a warm, inviting touch to the occasion. We had planned to chat and share a few drinks, our usual ritual for unwinding and catching up.

It was 5 p.m., when he arrived; however, he couldn't stay as he had urgent business to attend to. He left me a gift—a lovely bouquet of lilies, roses, and vibrant gerbera daisies. The lilies were pure white, their elegant form bringing a sense of grace, while the roses, in shades of soft blush and bright red, added a touch of warmth. The gerbera daisies, in cheerful yellow and orange, brought a bright pop of colour and a touch of playful charm.

He departed quickly, barely exchanging words, leaving me with a beautiful but bittersweet gift. His hasty exit left me feeling strangely deflated, the vibrant bouquet a poignant reminder of the fleeting nature of our meeting. "Psychiatrist" was a man whose calm, measured voice could soothe even the most agitated of souls, whose presence I had come to rely on deeply. He was a gentleman, always slow to speak but profound in his words, his quiet behaviour capable of calming even the birds with his soft-spoken encouragement.

Known to me for five years, he had become more of a close friend—someone who had significantly encouraged me to change careers and pursue my true calling. The warmth I had anticipated from our meeting seemed to dissipate, leaving me with a mix of disappointment and a longing for the support I so desperately needed at that moment.

I looked at myself in the mirror, determined not to let the evening's initial disappointment dictate my mood. With my makeup and hair done, I decided it would be a waste to stay in. It was a Thursday night, and the weather in London was unusually pleasant. The city seemed to hum with a different kind of energy, as if it too was encouraging me to step out and embrace the night. So, I called another dear friend, Suzan. She is a beautiful, tall woman with long, flowing blond hair that seemed to dance with every step she takes. She had a presence that commanded attention, and she always turned heads wherever she went. After a brief conversation, we decided to meet around 9 p.m. in Mayfair, central London.

By 7 p.m., I almost cancelled the plan. The anticipation was exhausting, and the familiar tug of anxiety had me second-guessing everything. Every minute felt like an eternity, and doubts began to creep in. But I reminded myself—this was exactly why I needed to socialise more, especially after the end of my last relationship. A relationship that, let's be honest, had been a challenge from day one, and I have never loved him. Deep down, I'd always known he wasn't the right fit for me. I mean, how long could I keep pretending it was fine to be with someone who didn't even share my taste in music? It sounds funny, but music has always been my guide, and I wasn't even listening to what I liked in my own house.

I was living in a space where the other person was content, while I was slowly becoming… well, unhappy. I reached a point where I realised enough was enough—I couldn't keep staying just to make someone else feel better. I wanted to be with someone who shared my values, my beliefs, my goals, my quirks, and yes, my playlist! Ending it wasn't easy, especially since he struggled to accept it. But I knew it was time to take that step, reclaim who I was, and chase my own happiness.

So, I shook off the nerves and decided tonight was the start of something new—something me. Determined to make the most of the evening, I left my flat at 7:30 p.m. and strolled through Green Park before meeting my friends. The park was a verdant oasis in the heart of the city, and I found solace in its quiet paths.

With my favourite music playing in my ears, I allowed myself to dream of a perfect life. I imagined meeting the man of my dreams, a man who would bring me back to life and support me to be the best version of myself, and the fun person I once was. My smile had faded way too much. I had been living in a state of numbness for a few years, unable to process my emotions and often ignoring them, leading me to feel a bit dry inside.

As I walked, I marvelled at the world around me. The trees swayed gently in the evening breeze, and the soft glow of the streetlamps cast a magical light on everything. I felt a glimmer of hope, a tiny spark that maybe, just maybe, things could change. After wandering in the park, I received a text from my friend Suzan she was running late.

I decided to stop for a meal at a cosy Polish restaurant in Shepherd Market, right in the heart of Mayfair. The place was charming, with rustic wooden tables and a warm, inviting atmosphere. The Polish beef goulash I ordered was a comforting blend of flavours, and it warmed my heart, evoking a sense of family and comfort. Each bite felt like a hug, reminding me of simpler times and the comfort of home-cooked meals.

Finally, Suzan arrived. She lit up the restaurant with her charisma. We shared a bottle of white wine, something I had turned to on and off in recent years as a way to numb my frustrations. The wine flowed, and with it, our conversations grew deeper and more meaningful. We talked about our dreams, our fears, and the things that kept us awake at night. As we neared the end of our meal, her friend Eros joined us. Eros was a tall, handsome man, funny and full of life and joy. He was one of the most attractive gay men I had ever met, and his vibrant energy was contagious. His laughter was infectious, and I felt a genuine smile spread across my face.

The evening was going smoothly, and I started to feel funny. I knew it was the reaction from the alcohol and me finally feeling free to enjoy my night. For a change, I wasn't thinking about being responsible. I actually wanted to have fun and let myself go that night without worrying about tomorrow. That carefree mindset made me accept my friends' invitation to go to a bar, something I usually declined.

Typically, I would come back home after dinner, never enjoying the night beyond 12 p.m. I always had it in mind that after midnight, people got drunk and a bit crazy. I tried to avoid those times to spare myself the dreadful hangover the next day, which always made me feel like dying. But that night, I wanted to feel alive. I didn't want to think about anything, especially not the hangover or any consequences. I just wanted to have fun with my friends.

We ended up going to a beautiful, new luxury restaurant in Mayfair, renowned for its amazing bar. As I was feeling tipsy, I found myself talking more than usual. Lately, I had become quite reserved, and alcohol had a way of making me forget my problems, making me more sociable. I had always enjoyed meeting people and having fun, but my private life had turned me into a cold person who rarely smiled. So, I used alcohol as an excuse to hide my pain and wear a fake happy mask. But, of course, that didn't last long. The next day, my body would react very badly, making me even more depressed and sad because it wasn't just the physical hangover, but the emotional pain mixed with guilt.

As we walked into the restaurant, we were greeted by a smiling waiter who kindly offered us the option to enjoy their private bar. The entrance was at the end of the restaurant in a dark corner, easily missed by someone who didn't know it existed. I opened the heavy, woody door and walked in, spotting a free table with three high stools. We settled there, and the waiter promptly came to ask what we would like to drink. I ordered my favourite cocktail at the time, a Porn Star Martini. The drinks arrived, and we toasted to joy and a great night. But I didn't know that my night was about to turn into a nightmare.

I got to sit down, feeling elegant with my beautiful Laura Piano flat shoes and wearing a cute, short (but not too short) white dress. My short, straight black hair was down, and I wore just enough makeup to feel pretty and sweet. Not even five minutes into the place, while I sat down, I noticed that I was about to give my back to a man seated right next to me. I turned and apologised for turning my back to him. He didn't hesitate to start a conversation with me after my comment.

He was tall, blonde, with green eyes, and had a strong Irish accent. We asked each other where we were from, and he told me he was from Ireland. The night started fine, but when he mentioned he was married, I didn't want any personal conversation but rather focused on talking about his job in IT, a field I was very interested in. We spent a long time speaking about technology and how AI is changing everything and everyone. The Irish man was very friendly, and we engaged well as we started laughing and telling jokes to each other, and the time seemed to fly.

The bar was nearing closing time, and everyone started mingling. We all decided to carry on the party somewhere else. We left the bar and walked to another bar nearby, trying to get the last few drinks as it was already past midnight—a time I always feared. I was not wrong because that's when everything started falling apart.

We didn't make it into the first bar we tried. The line was too long, and the bouncer looked like he wasn't in the mood to let anyone in. But the Irish guy, always quick on his feet, had an inside scoop. He leant in, lowering his voice as if sharing a secret, and told us he knew the doorman at a nearby nightclub.

"Trust me," he said, flashing a grin.

We decided to give it a shot. Sure enough, when we got there, we didn't even need to wait. Thanks to his connection, we waltzed right in like we owned the place. The music hit us as soon as we entered, pulsing through the walls, and a neon haze hung in the air.

He had somehow managed to secure a VIP table, too. Suzan and Eros exchanged excited looks, already buzzing with energy. Tonight was only just beginning.

Suzan was the kind of woman who could sip her drink with the precision of a surgeon. She'd barely had a few sips yet stayed sharp as a tack, eyes scanning the room like she was assessing every detail. Meanwhile, Eros and I were on an entirely different planet. We were so far gone that it felt like my feet had been replaced with fluffy pillows, and the floor beneath me shifted like a mirage.

Eros, on the other hand, was in his element. He danced like a pro, every move smooth and sensual, commanding the dance floor with a confidence that left everyone watching in awe. While I swayed and stumbled, trying to keep up, Eros moved with a grace that made it seem effortless. He was the embodiment of cool, his rhythm hypnotic, so much so that I almost forgot my own state of drunken bliss.

We were having the time of our lives—me, lost in a whirlwind of gleeful disarray, and Eros, turning every dance move into a masterclass in seduction. The night was a chaotic blend of his stunning performance and my joyful madness, a perfect balance of elegance and hilarity as we took over the dance floor.

Chapter 2
The Devil's Trap

In my moment of distraction, the devil stepped onto the dance floor—a seductive and alluring presence with a devilish grin. The pulsating music throbbed in my ears as this mysterious figure offered me a taste of cocaine. Despite my usual reservations, a surge of excitement coursed through me. The rush of adrenaline and the thrill of the unknown felt exhilarating, a sensation I had sorely missed.

In a wild and reckless moment, I succumbed to the temptation of the drugs, seeking escape in their potent embrace. The mixture of cocaine and alcohol ignited a fire within me, reigniting the dormant spark of adventure that had long lay dormant. The world around me blurred and twisted, the dance floor transforming into a stage for my inner desires to run wild.

The euphoria that followed was intoxicating—a heady cocktail of invincibility and liberation. I threw myself into the chaos of the night, shedding my inhibitions and embracing the darkness that simmered just beneath the surface. The devil's presence loomed large, whispering promises of ecstasy and danger in equal measure.

But as the night unfurled, the high began to wane, leaving behind a hollow emptiness that gnawed at my very soul. I found myself adrift in a sea of confusion and fear, the boundaries between reality and illusion blurring with each passing moment. In my quest for self-discovery, I had unwittingly plunged myself deeper into the abyss, losing myself in a whirlwind of chaos and desire.

As the first rays of dawn pierced through the darkness, illuminating the remnants of the night's revelry, I realised that I had danced with the devil and paid the price. The thrill of the chase had led me down a treacherous path, one from which there may be no return. The search for solace had only served to plunge me further into the depths of my own darkness, leaving me stranded in a night of illusion and despair.

In that moment of reckless abandon, the lines between fun and danger blurred. The nightclub's lights seemed to pulse in time with my racing heart, and the music became a hypnotic backdrop to the unfolding chaos. The Irish man, Eros, Suzan, and I danced wildly, laughing and shouting over the music, completely lost in our altered states.

My senses were heightened; every glance seemed amplified. The world outside the nightclub ceased to exist, and all that mattered was the thrill of the moment. But deep down, a part of me knew that I was teetering on the edge of a precipice, and the fall would be hard.

By 4 a.m., I felt like a completely different person—exhilarated and unwilling to let the night end. We were all drunk, some of us more than others, and the effects of everything we'd consumed made the idea of stopping unbearable. I suggested we keep the party going because the last thing I wanted was to be alone in this state. Normally, solitude wouldn't have bothered me, but the combination of drugs and alcohol left me feeling vulnerable, unprepared to face myself alone. Everyone agreed, and we decided to head to the Irish guy's hotel room.

We squeezed into a taxi, a tangle of limbs and laughter. When we arrived at the hotel, the receptionist stopped us, saying there were too many of us. Only Suzan and I were allowed in, leaving Eros behind. A sharp pang of frustration hit me—Eros had been with me all night, and we'd promised to end the night together, no matter what.

As Suzan and I dashed through the hotel's narrow, dimly lit corridors, my heart pounded in my chest, a growing unease settling over me. Eros lingered in my thoughts, his absence casting a shadow over the night. Something didn't feel right, and I couldn't shake the feeling that leaving him behind was a mistake.

With a sudden surge of determination, I grabbed Suzan's hand and made a split-second decision. "We need to go back," I said, breathless. "We have to find Eros." Without waiting for a response, I turned, dragging her with me as we raced down the stairs, our footsteps echoing through the empty hallways.

The urgency of the moment pushed us forward, each step carrying us closer to the truth waiting for us outside.

And then, we saw him—Eros, standing alone on the sidewalk, his expression a mixture of frustration and resignation. Without a second thought, I called out his name, the sound echoing through the stillness of the night. His face lit up with surprise and relief as we rushed toward him, pulling him into a tight embrace. The sense of reunion was overwhelming, a balm to the chaos that had unfolded inside.

The three of us, together again, decided it was time to head home. The cool night air cleared our heads, soothing our frayed nerves. As we called for a taxi, a strange peace settled over me, like a return to myself after the whirlwind of the night. Eros was safe, and in that moment, it felt like everything would be alright.

I ordered the taxi, set to arrive in four minutes. Despite feeling more grounded, I wasn't tired in the slightest. We lingered on the sidewalk, saying our goodbyes and reliving fragments of the night's madness. Then, out of nowhere, a voice broke the quiet: "Hello, wait!"

I turned to see the hotel receptionist sprinting toward us from the entrance, grinning like a kid who'd just pulled off a great prank. "I'll let you all in!" he announced triumphantly, clearly proud of himself.

I glanced up and saw the Irish guy waving from a first-floor window, completely on board with the plan. The street was dim, illuminated only by a few flickering streetlights. The warm night air clung to us like a second skin, the perfect setting for something ridiculous to happen.

I convinced my friends to give it another shot, telling them the night was still young. We walked back through the narrow, red-themed corridors of the hotel. The room we entered was surprisingly small, draped in red sheets and filled with vintage decor. A small table by the window caught my eye, and I quickly sat down. Eros, too drunk to stay awake, collapsed onto the bed, making me laugh when he landed with his butt sticking up in the air. The Irish guy sat beside him, facing me and the window, while Suzan wandered around, looking for a place to sit.

On the table, a collection of drinks sat unattended, their colours blending into the dim, moody lighting of the room. I poured myself a glass of red wine, but as soon as the sharp, sour smell hit my nose, my stomach twisted. A wave of nausea rolled through me, and I set the glass down, untouched. My thoughts were hazy, clouded by the events of the night, but I felt a deep pull to escape, to disconnect from the growing unease.

Without thinking, I made my way to the bathroom. The door clicked shut behind me, muffling the thumping bass that echoed outside.

I stared at my reflection in the mirror for a moment, my eyes wide, unblinking. Leaning over the sink, I found a small line of the drug left behind and, without hesitation, inhaled it. Almost instantly, it hit me—like a bolt of fire straight to my brain. My pupils dilated, and a surge of adrenaline shot through my body. The fight-or-flight instinct kicked in, reminding me of the danger I was toying with. But instead of running, I stood there, letting the intensity ripple through me, feeling my nerves light up in a way that was both thrilling and terrifying.

When I stepped back into the room, it felt as though I had entered another world. The faces around me blurred into a mass of shifting movement, the music thundering like an endless pulse, pounding in my skull. My heart raced, but amidst the chaos, one single, clear thought pierced through: I didn't want this.

"I'm not interested in anything physical," I blurted out, louder than I intended. My voice sliced through the noise, drawing a few curious glances. "Just conversation and music."

For a split second, the room seemed to freeze, a tension hanging in the air. Then, it eased. Suzan caught my eye and gave me a small nod. We'd agreed earlier to let the night flow with just music, nothing more. With that unspoken understanding, Suzan and I let ourselves drift into the rhythm, swaying together, allowing the music to guide us.

Behind us, Eros remained sprawled on the bed, dead to the world.

Time passed in a blur, each minute blending into the next. I couldn't tell how long we'd been there, but I could feel the atmosphere shifting, the energy building as the night wore on. The music grew louder, each beat pounding relentlessly, reverberating in my chest like a hammer. The bass was so heavy it felt like it was pressing down on me, suffocating me under its weight. It wasn't music anymore—it was a force, trapping me in this space, making my pulse race.

My heart thudded in my throat, my breath shallow as my skin began to burn. Every inch of me felt hot, as though my body had been set on fire from the inside. Sweat beaded on my forehead, and I wiped it away with the back of my hand, but the heat didn't stop. The room, once a haven of noise and distraction, now felt unbearably small. The air was thick, too warm, pressing in on me from every side. I couldn't hear the talking, the laughter—nothing but the deafening roar of my heartbeat and the music crashing through my head.

I couldn't stay any longer. I had to get out. I wasn't myself; I could feel it. Something had shifted. My laughter felt hollow, my smile stretched too wide, too forced. The music, once a background hum to our fun, now clawed at my senses, overwhelming me, drowning out any coherent thought.

I glanced down at my hands, and they were shaking. Violently. My fingers trembled as though they belonged to someone else. I could barely control them. That's when it hit me, hard and fast—the alcohol, the drug, the mix of it all. I had let myself slip, doing something I swore I'd never do. I didn't mind alcohol; it had become a familiar friend, a crutch that dulled the sharp edges of my thoughts. "But drugs? No." And yet, here I was, feeling the effects of a choice I hadn't even fully realised I'd made.

The laughter around me began to fade, as though someone had turned down the volume on the entire room. It was strange, eerie, like watching a scene through a fogged window. I could see mouths moving, people talking, but their voices felt distant, muted, as if they were coming from underwater. The room spun, the walls closing in.

I needed to get out. Now.

Panic rose in my chest, fast and fierce, and all I could think about escaped. I stood up abruptly, the ground beneath me wobbling as though it, too, was unsure of itself. I swayed for a moment, trying to find my balance, my vision blurring in and out of focus. The scent of stale beer, sweat, and something sharp—cigarettes, maybe—filled the air, mixing with the overwhelming smell of whatever cheap cologne. It made my stomach churn.

I glanced over at Eros, sprawled out on the bed like a corpse, completely unconscious. His face was slack, mouth slightly open, his chest rising and falling in slow, steady breaths. For a moment, I thought he was dead. I need to get out. I need to get him out.

"Wake up," I whispered, my voice tight with fear as I shook him a little harder than I intended. "Eros, wake up."

I looked around the room, desperate for help, and my eyes landed on Suzan. She was sitting nearby, her eyes locked on us with a look of concern, her brows furrowed as though she could sense that something was very wrong. She wasn't smiling anymore. I could see the question in her eyes before she even asked it.

"Are you okay?" she asked, her voice soft but tinged with worry.

I shook my head, the movement feeling sluggish, like I was underwater. "No," I replied, my voice shaky, barely audible over the fading music. "I need to leave."

Suzan didn't hesitate. She stood up quickly, coming over to me, her presence a strange comfort in the chaos of the moment. She could see it on my face—the fear, the desperation, the need to escape. Without a word, she bent down to try and rouse Eros, shaking him harder than I had dared to.

"Eros," she called, her voice firm, cutting through the dull roar of the room. "You need to get up. Now."

He jolted awake, his eyes flying open in shock, his body tense with confusion. He looked around, startled, his breath quickening as if trying to grasp where he was. We must have shaken him too hard—his face was a mix of fear and disorientation, like he'd just woken from a nightmare.

I could feel the bile rising in my throat, the room starting to spin again, faster this time. The smells around me—the alcohol, the cigarettes, the sweat—were too much. I felt trapped in this unfamiliar place. My mind screamed at me to run, to find silence, to be alone.

Stepping outside into daylight, I felt a wave of shame and guilt. People were heading to work as I was heading home, praying for sleep that seemed elusive. As we made our way through the dimly lit streets, the realisation of our reckless decisions began to weigh on me. The night, which had started with such excitement, had taken a turn I hadn't anticipated. I couldn't help but reflect on the series of events that had led us to this point.

The Irish guy, with his charismatic demeanour, had initially seemed like a fun distraction. The influence of substances had created a situation that was far from what I had intended. The hotel room, the atmosphere had been charged with a mix of exhilaration and apprehension. The vintage red décor and the small space for four people created an almost weird environment. I remembered the moment Eros had collapsed on the bed, his inebriated state contrasting sharply with the intensity of the situation. It had been both amusing and sobering, a reminder of how far we had strayed from our usual boundaries.

The reality of our situation became even clearer. The night had turned into morning, and the consequences of our actions were beginning to surface, intensified by the sight of people starting their day as I was ending mine. In the car, my thoughts raced. The anxiety was nearly overwhelming, and I had to fight the urge to abandon the ride and walk home. As I sat in the back of a taxi, my thoughts swirling into a storm of guilt, disappointment, and embarrassment, I couldn't help but feel judged, even by the silent cab driver, for returning home in such a scruffy state. My makeup had long since faded, leaving dark smudges around my eyes, which were now red and swollen. The harsh daylight felt like it was burning my retinas, each glance upwards causing me to squint and search the sky for a familiar face, someone who could offer comfort in my moment of despair.

As the taxi pulled up to my address, I scrambled out without so much as a thank you, overwhelmed by a profound sense of shame. My hands trembled as I fumbled for my keys, and I barely managed to press the button for the lift. Inside, the mirror reflected a version of myself that was almost unrecognisable—eyes bloodshot and filled with loneliness, a mask of sadness staring back at me. I had known this would happen the moment I decided to stay out, allowing myself to be swept away by the night. The drugs, however, were an unexpected and harsh catalyst, pushing me to the brink.

The disconnect between my current state and the world around me was stark. Arriving home, the burden of the night's events weighed heavily on me. The excitement that had initially driven us to continue the party had long dissipated, leaving behind a lingering sense of regret.

Chapter 3
A Dance with Death

The morning of June 28th dawned on me with an unforgiving brightness. Arriving home around 8 a.m., I replayed the night's events in my mind. The initial excitement at the club, the decision to go to the hotel, the discomfort of leaving Eros behind, the surreal atmosphere of the hotel room, and the eventual realisation of our reckless behaviour. It was a night that had promised so much but had ultimately left me feeling more disconnected and lost than before.

The morning light streaming through the window was a stark reminder of the reality I had to face. The night had been a whirlwind of emotions and experiences, but now it was time to confront the physical pain, which I was fine with, but not the emotional consequences. While I had always been ready to face physical pain, emotional pain was something I had long hidden and avoided.

I couldn't even muster the energy to shower or wash my face. Instead, I grabbed a bottle of water and drank until I felt I might drown. Collapsing onto my bed, I desperately tried to calm my racing mind and erase the memories of the night. But every time I closed my eyes, I was bombarded by flashes of light and the relentless thump of music. Tossing and turning, I found no solace, no escape from my own thoughts.

As I drifted into uneasy sleep, I couldn't help but wonder how I would reconcile the person I had been that night with the person I wanted to become. The journey back to myself would be long, but it was a path I knew I had to take.

It was hard to stay in bed, so in a desperate attempt to find some relief, I took a few tablets to help me sleep and drew a cold bath, hoping the chill might soothe my overheated body.

As I lay in the water, my body began to feel strange—numb, disconnected. Unease washed over me, and I decided to get out.

I went back to bed, still damp, but the anxiety crept back in almost immediately. Sleep was elusive, taunting me with its promise but never arriving.

Desperate for distraction, I reached for my phone, hoping it might calm my mind. Instead, the texts and photos from the night flashed across the screen, sending my heart into a frenzy. My body trembled uncontrollably. I was convinced I was going to die right there. Time dragged on endlessly, amplifying my frustration and fear.

Misery drove me to turn on the TV, hoping the noise and images might drown out my thoughts. But instead of easing the tension, it began to rise, like a storm brewing inside me. My heart started racing, pounding too fast for comfort. My breathing grew shallow, and panic clawed at me. I knew I had to do something to stop the spiral.

I jumped into a hot shower, hoping the heat would soothe me. But instead, a strange tingling spread across my tongue. My body began to feel cold, shaking uncontrollably. My legs went numb, and I found myself sinking down into the bath, my skin prickling with an icy chill. I couldn't feel my tongue anymore, and my eyelids grew heavy, like weights pulling me into darkness.

I fainted. I don't know how long I lay there, unconscious beneath the water. When I finally came to, panic gripped me like a vice, a crushing fear as if I had died and somehow clawed my way back. My lips were numb, a strange, tingling cold spreading across them. As I gasped for air, they felt stiff, almost foreign to me, like they didn't belong to my body anymore.

I scrambled out of the bath, my legs weak and shaking beneath me. My hands, trembling violently, fumbled as I switched off the water. The room spun around me, my vision blurring at the edges. My body felt drained, hollowed out, as though every ounce of life had been siphoned away while I lay submerged.

My skin was cold, clammy, my breath coming in shallow, ragged bursts. The air in the room was thick, suffocating, pressing down on me like a weight I couldn't escape. My lungs burnt, desperate for fresh air. I needed to get out—anything to break free from the heavy, oppressive atmosphere in the flat, before the darkness claimed me again.

I had to get out. I craved the comfort of being near someone, anyone, just to feel a human presence beside me. But I couldn't bring myself to do it. The shame was too heavy, too suffocating. The guilt of it burnt inside me like a brand. The thought of being around anyone, of letting them see me like this, filled me with dread. "How could I face anyone when I could barely face myself?" The idea of reaching out, of asking for help, felt impossible. I didn't want to see their disappointment, their worry—I couldn't bear it.

So, instead, I decided on something where I wouldn't have to speak, where no one would expect me to explain the mess I was in—a massage. It was a way to be touched, to be cared for, without the shame of having to confess why I needed it. It was my only option, a way to feel human again without exposing just how far I'd fallen.

I booked the appointment at a place just across the road. When I stepped outside, the daylight felt like needles against my skin, and my eyes stung as if filled with sand. I forced myself to keep walking, pulling sunglasses over my pale face, hiding the redness in my eyes. I tried to wear the mask of someone suffering from mere illness, hoping no one would look too closely.

The massage was gentle, each touch a small relief to the tangled nerves beneath my skin. Little by little, the tension ebbed, like the hands were pulling me back from the edge. For a brief hour, I wasn't drowning in shame or panic. I could breathe again.

When I got home, I didn't even think about eating—my stomach was too knotted, too unsettled. All I could do was crawl into bed, hoping sleep would come and offer me some escape from the weight pressing down on my chest.

Finally, I managed to fall into a fitful sleep, my body and mind exhausted. When I woke it was only 10 p.m., with the insistent buzz of notifications on my phone. Family and friends were trying to reach me, but I couldn't face them. I silenced the device and lay back down, praying for strength and health. As I drifted back to sleep, I clung to the hope that Saturday would bring a fresh start, that I would wake feeling alive and capable once more.

Chapter 4
A Desperate Kind of Hope

Saturday morning arrived with a sense of renewal, the kind that drapes itself over you like a warm blanket after a long night. The early light filtered into my room, gentle yet insistent, as if nudging me back to myself. I opened my eyes, feeling a strange clarity—my body lighter, my mind clearer, and yesterday's confusion settling into a distant memory. It felt surreal, as though I had survived a test I didn't even know I was taking. Quietly, I whispered a thank you, feeling grateful for this unexpected second chance.

I shifted, stretching in bed, and a wave of resolve washed over me. Today, I knew, was about facing myself and the choices that had brought me here. Steeling myself, I went to take a long shower, letting the warm water pour over me, scrubbing my skin as though washing away more than just the scents of alcohol and stale perfume. The steam swirled around me, heavy with the memories I was trying to cleanse. As I rinsed away the suds, I felt lighter, as if part of the burden I carried was being washed down the drain.

Stepping out, I caught a glimpse of my reflection in the mirror, fogged but still discernible. My face looked softer; my eyes less swollen. There was something there—a small but unmistakable spark reminding me, "You're still here. You're still you." The memory of my heart racing wildly the night before flickered in my mind, but I pushed it aside. I couldn't—no, wouldn't—let that feeling pull me back.

I powered on my phone, and it immediately buzzed with a string of missed calls. My friends had been trying to reach me. Of course they're worried, I thought, my finger hovering over Suzan's name. Quickly, I sent her a short message: "I'm okay. I'll call later." It wasn't that I didn't want to talk—I just wasn't ready to relive it, not yet. Today, I needed to hold space for myself.

Then I saw another name: him. The Irish guy. My heart skipped, betraying me, but I pushed it down. Before I could think too much, I swiped left, deleting his messages without even opening them, and blocked his number. The screen went blank, a quiet finality settling over me.

Scrolling through more messages, I came to the ones from my family. There was one from my mother, warm and simple, just checking in. My fingers shook as I typed out a reply, assuring her I was fine, blaming it all on a late night out with friends. Her response came quickly—a laughing emoji that softened my guilt, though it didn't erase it. I could almost picture her reading my message, imagining a carefree night, none the wiser about the mess I'd actually stumbled into.

The weekend passed slowly. The house was silent, the tick of the clock breaking the stillness, every second stretching longer than the last. Anxiety simmered under my skin, a dull ache that wouldn't quite fade. I stayed in bed, my mind replaying the fragments of that night, each memory like a jagged piece of glass I couldn't avoid. I could still feel the weight of my choices pressing on me, a steady, relentless reminder of what I needed to change.

Each hour brought a new wave of regret, a heaviness settling in my chest. Questions swirled, like echoes of doubt: "Why had I let myself spiral? Why did I let myself become this?" It wasn't who I wanted to be, wasn't the life I wanted. And yet, I had allowed myself to fall, let myself lose control in ways I couldn't ignore.

I felt broken, and yet, beneath the fatigue and regret, a tiny spark of resolve was urging me on. From now on, it would be different, even if I didn't fully believe it yet. My life lately had left me feeling stripped bare, my spirit raw and aching. I had been sinking, and I knew I couldn't do this alone anymore.

But then, in the quiet, a thought surfaced—soft but unmistakable, like a small light flickering in the dark. I need something bigger than myself. I needed an anchor, something steady to guide me back to solid ground. And for the first time in so long, I thought of faith—not as a distant idea, but as a lifeline, a hope. It was the one thing I hadn't reached for in the chaos, yet it felt like the only thing that could truly hold me steady.

The realisation felt like a quiet kind of epiphany, a sense that maybe this was how I could return to myself. Faith could be my guide, a love stronger than the momentary highs, something that could remind me of who I truly was beneath the scars, the mistakes, the regrets. And with that thought, a sense of calm settled over me, bringing with it the promise of a new beginning.

Chapter 5
In God's Grace: Seeking Answers and a Wish for Love

Monday morning, the 8th of July, dawned with a sense of quiet resolve as I embarked on my journey back to self-awareness and responsibility. The harrowing experiences of the previous twelve days, reflecting on myself and my unhealthy behaviours, have etched themselves deeply into my consciousness, teaching me invaluable lessons about my limits, the dangers of excess, and the paramount importance of self-respect. I vowed to distance myself from situations that compromised my values and principles, knowing that I deserved far better than the self-destructive path I had been on.

With a renewed sense of purpose and determination, I approached the new week with a clear vision. The nightmare of the past twelve days was behind me, and with what I hoped was God's grace, I looked forward to a brighter, more balanced future. The first step was to address the practical matters that had been left in disarray. I went through my morning routine methodically—shower, hair styled, and dressed in my best—before heading to the bank to resolve the issues with my account after extravagance on shopping and night outs. The relief of having my financial situation resolved and everything cleared felt like a small but significant victory, a step toward reclaiming my stability.

As I left the bank, a crucial part of my plan for the day lay ahead: a visit to the church. This wasn't just a casual stop; it was a pilgrimage of sorts, a desperate conversation with God about everything I had endured and how I was ready to leave behind the old me—the one who had strayed from her true self over the past years. I made my way to a beautiful church in Holland Park, a place that had long been my sanctuary, a refuge where I had sought solace and clarity during turbulent times. This church had seen me in my darkest moments, on my knees, asking for guidance and support.

But today was different. Today, I entered with an open heart, ready to confront my past and embrace the future. I approached the altar with a profound sense of vulnerability, kneeling down and pouring out my soul. I asked God for forgiveness for all my sins, for every wrong turn and misstep. The most poignant of my pleas was for forgiveness for having neglected myself.

I had been so harsh, so unkind to me, letting my happiness slip away and allowing myself to be let down. I sought forgiveness for any harm I may have caused others, for staying in a relationship fundamentally damage. I was desperate for absolution, for a fresh start.

I continued my fervent plea, my voice trembling with emotion. Despite a deep-seated belief that leaving my last relationship was the right choice, doubt still lingcrcd in my mind, cvcn knowing being in it was so wrong seemed right at that moment.

"Please, God," I implored:

"Show me if I made the right decision. Help me see, was I right to end my previews relationship? Did I make the right choice? If the answer is yes, then send me a sign. Make my eyes see the truth, and I promise I will follow the signs and understand the message. I am ready to receive the answer to my question, trusting my life in Your hands. With a commitment to embracing the truth and moving forward to my purpose, I vow to be kind and loyal to my true self."

Kneeling on the cold, hard floor of the dimly lit church, I felt utterly vulnerable. The distant echo of footsteps and the soft rustle of pages being turned filled the sacred space, adding to the weight of my emotions.

"I believe that only You, God, can truly change my life. With Your help, I vow to encourage myself each day to become a better person and to be the best version of myself. Please forgive me for all my sins, for the unnecessary pain I allowed myself to endure, and for the hurt I have caused others. I no longer want to live the life I am living or be the person I am now. I surrender myself to You for transformation."

With a pure heart, I asked if "I deserved to be happy with someone, send me someone who will show me what love is, someone who will teach me how to love, someone who I will allow myself to love deeply." I have always believed my true love was somewhere out there, searching for me.

"God," I whispered, my voice trembling, "I assure You; I am ready to welcome him into my life—a perfect partner who aligns with my values and dreams. I promise to be ready to receive him, ready to embrace a new life and purpose to be happy again."

The smell of incense lingered in the air, and the flickering candlelight cast shadows that danced across the walls. Tears streamed down my face, each one a desperate plea from the depths of my soul. The weight of uncertainty pressed heavily on my heart, but I clung to the hope that a sign would guide me. As the silence enveloped me, I searched for a whisper of reassurance, a flicker of light to pierce the darkness of my doubt.

As I prayed, I envisioned the kind of man I hoped to find. The soft hum of the church's heating system and the distant, muffled voices of other worshippers created a tranquil backdrop, grounding me in the moment.

I longed for someone who shared my values and lifestyle—a family-oriented man, dedicated to his career and personal goals. Someone driven, focused on success, even if it meant having little free time. I yearned for someone free from addiction, who abstained from cigarettes and alcohol, and who shared my passion for fitness and wellness—a passion I had lost somewhere along the way but was ready to rekindle.

As I lay there, I made a quiet promise to myself: I would return to that passion as my first step toward change, my first promise of becoming the person I wanted to be. I wanted a love that matched my ideals, but I knew I had to start by being the kind of person who would naturally attract it.

I imagined his presence as a comforting solidity, someone who could reignite my passion for life. I desired a man whose heart was as kind as mine, someone who would love me for who I truly am, just as I would love him.

In my mind's eye, I pictured a man who could appreciate the playful side of me—the woman who loved to laugh, tell jokes, dance, and lose herself in rock and roll. I could almost hear the infectious laughter, the sound of our favourite songs playing in the background, the rhythm of our footsteps dancing across the floor.

I sought a partner who was just a little older than me, someone ready for commitment, proud to walk by my side, and capable of expressing love through words, touches, and meaningful actions—not just words alone. I envisioned someone who would actively support my dreams and aspirations, share in life's joys and challenges, and demonstrate his affection through small, thoughtful gestures that reflected his deep understanding of me.

This was the man I envisioned, a reflection of what I once was and what I wanted to become again. The vision of him filled me with a warmth that contrasted with the chill of the stone floor beneath my knees. The flickering candles cast a golden glow, their light dancing on the polished wooden pews, and I felt a renewed sense of hope. With every heartbeat, the image of this man grew clearer, a beacon of love and companionship that I was ready to embrace.

As the minutes ticked by in the serene atmosphere of the church, I felt a shift within myself. The soft, distant echoes of whispered prayers and the faint rustle of clothing as people shifted in their seats added to the sacred stillness. The scent of incense lingered in the air, mingling with the faint mustiness of old wood and stone. My heart, once heavy with past regrets and uncertainties, began to lighten. The weight of my past missteps seemed to ease, replaced by a tentative hope for the future. I knew that finding this man would not be an instant fix, but it was a beacon of hope, a sign that the journey I was on could lead to something profoundly fulfilling.

I left the church with a sense of clarity and peace, the cool air outside brushing against my cheeks, invigorating my senses. The future was no longer an intimidating void but a canvas waiting to be painted with the vibrant colours of my aspirations. The texture of the cobblestones under my feet and the distant hum of city life reminded me of the world waiting just beyond my prayers. As I walked away, I carried with me a newfound resolve, eager to embrace the destiny I had prayed for and to leave behind the shadows of my past.

Chapter 6
Revelation in the Streets
God's Unspoken Answer

Walking down Holland Park, the sounds of bustling traffic and the chatter of pedestrians filled the air. The aroma of freshly brewed coffee wafted from nearby cafes, blending with the crisp, cool air. My footsteps echoed lightly against the pavement, each step a reminder of the journey ahead. I got busy on my phone, the bright screen contrasting with the overcast sky. Lost in the digital world, I found myself veering off course, the rhythmic click of my heels on the pavement gradually leading me farther from the station than I'd intended. Perhaps I subconsciously wanted to prolong my walk, to breathe in the fresh air and reflect on the profound conversation I had just had with God. For the first time in a long while, I had borne my soul, asking for guidance and forgiveness.

The street around me was alive with activity, but I felt a serene detachment, as if floating through a dream. The vibrant storefronts and the gentle sway of trees lining the street seemed more vivid, each detail sharpened by the clarity I felt within. My heart swelled with a quiet joy, each breath a promise of renewal. As I navigated the streets, I was filled with a profound sense of purpose, ready to embrace whatever lay ahead.

As I strolled down a narrow road, my thoughts were interrupted by a loud, boisterous laugh. It was a woman's laugh, so hearty and uninhibited that it immediately grabbed my attention. I wasn't the only one; a man riding a bicycle towards me also turned his head to the left, seemingly curious about the source of the laughter. I continued walking, the sound growing louder and more distinct. As I rounded a corner, I couldn't believe what my eyes were seeing.

There, parked on the side of the road, was my ex's car. The laughter was coming from a woman inside, and through the windshield, I could see them both sharing a moment of pure joy. They looked carefree and happy, the picture of contentment. In that instant, I knew this was God's answer to my prayer, the question I had asked just half an hour ago. I couldn't contain myself and looked up at the skies, thanking God for showing me the truth so clearly and so swiftly. At that moment, I felt truly heard and grateful for never losing my faith and hope.

For a moment, I stood there, frozen, as a whirlwind of emotions surged through me—betrayal, anger, sadness—all clashing inside, and I was ready to face. Despite being the one who chose to break away, I felt a profound sense of sadness. I was disappointed in myself for the years I had wasted in a relationship where I had stopped feeling anything. Yet, I had dragged myself through years in an empty partnership, locking away my feelings and emotions, moving through life on autopilot, focusing only on my job and not interested in anything new.

After that frozen moment, I decided to walk past them. I could barely hear my heart pounding in my chest as my cold gaze locked onto his eyes. I made sure he could see, without a single word, that this was the end—the end of doubt and the end of the woman who had been hidden for so long.

As I continued down the road, a silent prayer formed in my mind, asking God to keep him away from me. I didn't want to hear his voice, see his face, or feel his presence. The farther I walked, the lighter I felt. My mind began to clear, my heart lifted, and I felt a new sense of freedom. The sky seemed brighter, the air crisper, and for the first time in what felt like ages, I felt a surge of positive energy. In less than half an hour, I had undergone a transformation. I felt reborn, my soul rejuvenated, my spirit revitalised.

The sensation was unbelievably unique, something that words could hardly describe. It was as if my wounds started healing at an incredible speed, and the pain of the last few years began to fade away. As I made my way home, I felt like my feet weren't even touching the ground. The thoughts fighting in my head and the voices that had been tormenting me grew quiet. All I could hear was my heart beating steadily and the slow, calming breath coming out from my mouth. The realisation hit me like a bolt of lightning: yes, I had been right to end the relationship. Seeing them together was the confirmation I needed. It was as if God was showing me the truth I had been avoiding, the undeniable proof that moving on was the best decision I could have made.

When I finally arrived home, I grabbed my phone with a sense of finality. I blocked his number, deleting his presence from my life and my mind. I gathered everything he had ever given me and put it all in a rubbish bag. I took the bag to the bin, and with each step, I felt a weightlifting off my shoulders. This marked the beginning of my self-realisation. I felt an overwhelming sense of freedom. I remembered telling my mum once that I was a free spirit in my early 20s, yet I had imprisoned myself for far too long. Now, finally, I was free and happy again. I knew and believed that the best was yet to come. A new book of my life was about to start, and I was going to be again the driver of my life this time. I was ready to steer my life towards a future filled with hope, joy, and endless love.

Chapter 7
Aligning with the Universe

The dawn of a new day broke like any other, but an unspoken anticipation hung in the air. The previous day, I had a profound conversation with God. I prepared for my morning routine. There was an unfamiliar sense of purpose in every step I took, a feeling that today would be different. As I stepped into the shower, an intense heat spread through my body, so powerful that I wondered if I was falling ill or running a fever. My blood felt like it was boiling beneath my skin. Desperate to cool down, I switched to cold water, yet it still felt warm against my heated skin.

Immersed in the fruity and chamomile scents of my shower gel, I felt a profound sense of presence. For the first time, I experienced the cold water in a new way, every droplet heightening my senses. With my eyes closed, I became attuned to the world outside—the rustling wind, the chirping birds, and the faint strains of music I had played in the background. Music, once my teenage refuge, now filled me with a wave of nostalgia and clarity. Positivity exuded from every pore, my soul illuminating me from within. I began to have vivid visions of my path ahead, as if a television screen in my mind was guiding me with crystal-clear images.

Determined to prioritise the most important person in my life—"Me"—I embarked on my workout with renewed vigour. My day unfolded smoothly, and on a whim, I decided to book a hairdresser appointment. I wanted to reclaim the beautiful face and captivating smile that everyone had once admired but I had forgotten. As I underwent my transformation, the change was remarkable. My pale skin took on a healthy glow, and my tired eyes sparkled with a vibrant energy that seemed to hypnotise those around me. My superpower was back, and as I walked down the street, I noticed the intrigued and admiring looks from strangers. I felt the universe aligning with me, conspiring to help me achieve my dreams.

Following my workout, I had an appointment to get my lashes done. This was part of my commitment to bringing out the best version of myself, not just in appearance but in how I felt inside. I realised the profound importance of inner happiness, understanding that feeling good on the inside is just as crucial as looking good on the outside. Happiness is a force within us, and I was determined to let nothing prevent me from presenting my best self to the world. My past experiences had been necessary lessons, paving the way for a new and stronger me.

After getting my lashes done, I moved on to a manicure and pedicure. I chose white for my nails—my second favourite colour—symbolising the clarity and purity of my thoughts.

As the day drew to a close, I took a quiet moment to breathe deeply and pray, feeling grateful for the resilience that had carried me through so many storms. When I returned home, I sank into a comfortable corner of my room, letting the warmth of the space settle around me. The setting sun cast a soft, golden glow across the room, filling it with a serene beauty that matched my growing sense of peace. Stoicism, introduced to me by my older brother, had become my guiding philosophy—a steady anchor through turbulent times.

I let my mind drift back to the wisdom of ancient thinkers like Marcus Aurelius and Seneca, names that now resonated with a depth I hadn't fully appreciated until now. Each line felt like a balm for my soul, comforting and familiar. I recalled Marcus Aurelius' words: "You have power over your mind—not outside events. Realise this, and you will find strength." It was a reminder that strength could be quiet, like the steady beating of a heart, and that it began from within.

To fortify my mind, I promised myself to make meditation part of my daily rhythm, a ritual that would ground me in the present moment. I imagined each breath as a wave, washing away any lingering doubts or anxieties. I could already feel the calm rising within me, each inhale and exhale becoming a quiet sanctuary. And long walks in nature would be my way to nourish my spirit—crisp air filling my lungs, rustling leaves whispering their secrets, the scent of damp earth anchoring me in the beauty surrounding me.

As I reflected on these ancient words, I let them fill my heart, their wisdom becoming my guide toward resilience and inner peace. Each lesson was a stepping stone, encouraging me to rise above life's uncertainties and embrace whatever was to come. I felt a new strength blooming inside me, a gentle but determined confidence that maybe, just maybe, I was exactly where I needed to be.

With faith renewed, I understood that my journey was only beginning. Stoicism reminded me that while my past had shaped me, it did not define me. My heart was ready to let go of what I couldn't control and to focus on the only things I truly held power over: my thoughts and my actions. And with each step, I would become more resilient, more aligned with my purpose of becoming the best version of myself.

Each night, as I closed my eyes, I would carry with me a quiet sense of peace, ready to greet the morning with open arms and an open heart. I would live fully, embracing whatever came my way with grace and hope. This awakening wasn't just a moment—it was the start of a journey of self-discovery, empowerment, and unwavering faith in my ability to grow.

I would forge ahead with purpose, dedicated to becoming the person I was meant to be, embracing every opportunity and challenge along the way. Each day would be a step closer to my best self, a journey that would lead me to a life filled with meaning, fulfilment, and an unwavering belief in my potential.

Chapter 8
An Unexpected Encounter

Thursday morning, the 11th of July. The sun streamed through my window, casting a warm glow on the scattered items in my flat. As I prepared to leave, the scent of freshly brewed coffee from the kitchen mingled with the crisp morning air that wafted in. Realising I was running late for my gym class, I hurried down the long, narrow staircase. Each step echoed in the stairwell, a rhythmic reminder of my urgency. At the bottom, I greeted the reception staff, a dark-skinned man with a slender build who always had a warm smile on his face. His cheerful “Good morning!” was a brief yet pleasant interruption, but it added to my delay.

Torn between walking as I normally do or taking the bus to save time, I decided on the latter, hoping it would mitigate the consequences of my tardiness. Typically, I enjoyed my 30-minute walk to the gym, relishing the routine of listening to music, reorganising my thoughts, or immersing myself in YouTube videos about stoicism. The rhythmic tapping of my shoes against the pavement usually provided a comforting background to my reflections. But as I stepped outside, the bright sunlight illuminated my oversight—I had left my EarPods behind.

With no time to spare, I headed left to the bus stop instead of my usual right. The street was alive with the sounds of a city morning: the distant hum of traffic, the occasional honk of a car horn, and the chatter of people starting their day. The sidewalks were bustling with commuters, their faces a blur of determination and distraction. The sun was shy on my face, the light creating a kaleidoscope of colours as it filtered through the leaves of the trees lining the street. Each step I took felt urgent, the texture of the concrete beneath my feet grounding me in the moment.

Despite the rush, I felt an overwhelming sense of joy and gratitude. I was blessed and lucky for everything I had: the supportive family, the beautiful people God had placed in my life. Reaching the bus stop, I checked my phone to see how long the wait would be. The bus was running late, and instead of succumbing to anxiety, I decided to use the time wisely. I went through my emails and watched funny videos online, filling my mind with positive thoughts and laughter. I was determined to enjoy my day and embrace any challenges with grace and courage.

As I waited for the bus, I lost myself in my phone, the digital world a distraction from my racing thoughts. Suddenly, a male voice cut through my reverie, resonating deeply, almost vibrating through my core. Startled, I looked up, and there he was. He had jumped in front of me with the agility of a cat, wearing a hat that partially obscured his face. But it was his deep, cat-like eyes and the fine wrinkles around them that captivated me. His gaze seemed to penetrate my soul, a mix of warmth and intrigue.

Normally, I would've brushed off any stranger trying to talk to me, like I always do. But this moment felt different. It was as if God Himself had arranged the situation, trapping me in a place where I couldn't run away. And this man, he wasn't just any man. There was something in his eyes, a connection I couldn't explain, and no matter how much I wanted to ignore him, I simply couldn't resist.

He appeared at ease, clad in a cosy, well-worn sweatshirt and track pants that hinted at a casual morning routine. It seemed as though he had effortlessly thrown on his outfit, not concerned with the opinions of others, simply embracing his laid-back, carefree demeanour. It was almost as if he had just rolled out of bed and decided to venture out, unconcerned with his appearance, embodying a sense of "stress-free" masculinity. His relaxed attitude exuded a sense of comfort, a man comfortable in his own skin. I paid little attention to his attire, neither did I, as I dressed in my sleek black gym outfit, eager for a workout without worrying about appearing unkempt and sweaty in the gym.

As I observed him, I couldn't help but notice the cup of coffee in his hand, likely from one of my beloved local coffee spots, indicating that he was a familiar face in the neighbourhood. His blond and grey beard accentuated his features, drawing my gaze to his lips, curved in a genuine and captivating smile. The sight of his smile stirred a warmth within me, causing a gentle blush to colour my cheeks. Feeling a mix of shyness and surprise, I discreetly surveyed him, taking note in his solid build and the gentle confidence in his posture.

Seeing the cup of coffee made my heart skip a beat. I loved coffee, and the aroma wafting from his cup was tantalising, adding another layer of attraction.

The rich, comforting scent mixed with the fresh morning air, creating a sensory experience that heightened the moment. His choice of coffee from my favourite shop felt like a sign, a small yet significant connection that made me feel even more drawn to him.

He seemed happy, his face radiating a kindness that made my heart flutter. His slow gestures as he approached me were deliberate and gentle, as if he wanted to savour the moment as much as I did. The sound of birds chirping filled the air, their melodies creating a serene backdrop to our meeting. The street, usually bustling with activity, felt unusually quiet and peaceful, as if the world had paused just for us. Nobody else seemed to be around, adding to the intimacy of the moment.

He asked if I had a boyfriend, and I replied, *"No, not anymore."* His follow-up question, "Why?" left me momentarily speechless. I felt a mix of emotions: a wave of realisation and happiness at being single again, yet a twist of frustration at having to revisit the past. I simply said, *"Long story."* His response was comforting, "Everyone has a past. Would you like to chat over a coffee with me?" Without hesitation, I agreed, though I tried to hide my excitement.

Handing him my phone, he dialled his number and called me back. I noticed his hands shaking slightly as he explained, "I look a bit better than this," sensing he might be worried about being judged by his appearance. I found it endearing that his hands were trembling; it showed vulnerability and courage. I knew I could be intimidating to men, and I valued his bravery in approaching me.

We exchanged a few more words before he politely asked me to text him on WhatsApp. I nodded and watched as he walked away, his steps measured and deliberate. Sitting there at the bus stop, I quickly saved his name in my phone: "Gato bus stop." Little did I know that this brief encounter would be the beginning of an unimaginable journey.

The day passed in a blur of responsibilities. I returned home late, exhausted but with a lingering excitement from the morning. Before making dinner, I decided to text Gato, "Hello, it's me, the girl from the bus stop." To my surprise, he replied almost immediately. We exchanged a few messages, but something about his profile picture intrigued me. It seemed familiar, yet not quite like the man I had met. I chose not to mention it.

As it was late, our conversation was brief, ending with a mutual "Good Night." Despite the short exchange, I felt good about it. Lying in bed, I looked at his photo again, trying to place where I had seen that face before. The picture didn't exactly match my memory of him, but it didn't bother me much.

Then, a wave of excitement washed over me as I remembered my upcoming trip to Barcelona. I had booked flights to visit a friend and spend a few days on the beach, soaking up the sun and getting some much-needed vitamin D. As I drifted off to sleep, I felt a sense of anticipation for both the trip and the possibilities with Gato.

The next morning, I woke up with a renewed sense of energy and purpose. The memory of Gato's eyes lingered in my mind, like a whisper of a dream that fades but leaves an impression. I spent the day in a heightened state of anticipation, each moment imbued with a subtle, thrilling undercurrent. I tried to immerse myself in my routine, but my thoughts kept drifting back to him.

When the evening came, my phone buzzed with a new text message. I assumed it was from my family, as they were the only ones who usually texted me at that hour. Without much thought, I picked up my phone and saw his name flash across the screen: Gato bus stop. My heart leaped at the sight of his name, and for a moment, I could almost hear it echo the sound of the text alert.

I opened the message with a mixture of excitement and curiosity. He asked, "How was your day?" A simple question, yet it felt loaded with promise. Our conversation flowed naturally. I couldn't contain my curiosity any longer and asked, "Have we ever met before? I feel like I've seen you somewhere."

I hesitated, then added, "Could it be from a dating app or something?" But then I quickly remembered that I don't use dating apps as "I can't judge people by pictures. I prefer the old-fashioned way, being out and about, meeting people face to face."

Gato's response was thoughtful. "If we've crossed paths somewhere, I would remember you."

As our conversation deepened, he asked, "Do you have any plans for the weekend?"

I remembered I had a flight to catch to Barcelona. Part of me hoped he was hinting at an invitation for coffee, but I couldn't make it that weekend. *"I'm flying to Barcelona,"* I replied, trying to sound casual. *"But I'll be back on Tuesday."*

"That sounds amazing! Have a great time, I love Barca," he texted back. "Maybe we can grab a coffee or a drink when you're back. Also, I know the best burger place." As I assumed, he was a burger lover.

"I'm not as much into burgers," I confessed. "I prefer fish and chicken. I eat a lot of chicken and vegetables since I'm focusing on my health."

"That sounds good too," he replied with enthusiasm.

Our conversation ended with mutual wishes for a good night and an unspoken promise hanging in the air. The thought of meeting him in person made my heart race with a blend of excitement and nervous anticipation. As I drifted off to sleep, I imagined what our meeting would be like. Would it be as easy and natural as our conversations? Would the connection I felt through the screen translate into real life?

I couldn't remember the last time I went for a coffee with someone I genuinely wanted to be with. The thought crossed my mind—could this be a date? However, it felt less stressful to view it simply as a coffee outing. As I lay in bed, I could hear my own voice in my head speaking enthusiastically to me. I felt my eyes smiling and the corners of my lips forming a discreet yet happy and sweet smile on my face. The faint aroma of lemongrass from my bedside diffuser enveloped me in a sense of calm.

As I replayed our conversation in my mind, I chuckled at a particularly funny moment. He had asked me, out of the blue, if I liked burgers. Why not anything else? Why burgers? Was he hungry? Did I look hungry? I laughed to myself, realising that was the moment the fun part of me—the part that had been dormant—started to wake up. His unexpected question and the light-hearted banter that followed made me feel more alive and excited than I had in a long time.

Chapter 9
Saturday Flight to Barcelona

There I was, preparing myself for a weekend away, making my way to Gatwick Airport, feeling light and free. For the first time, I was travelling with a positive and joyful spirit, not having to answer endless calls and text messages or explain where I was going and who I was with. The sense of freedom made my blood rush, warming my body. I felt my cheeks flush with excitement, and it was as if lights were radiating from within me. All I could think about was how wonderful it felt to be alive again, no longer lost in the negative thoughts that had dragged me down and made me feel old and weak.

As I walked to the lounge, where I would typically indulge in wine or champagne, I opted for still water, salad, and fruits. The crispness of the greens and the sweetness of the fruit were a refreshing change. I observed the people around me, each engrossed in their phones or laptops, hardly looking up. Everyone was in their own world, but I was there, drinking my water and watching the planes land and take off. The hum of the airport, the distant chatter, and the clinking of glasses created a symphony of sounds that heightened my senses.

I remembered my childhood desire to be free, unencumbered by anyone or anything, yearning for new adventures. The memory of arriving in London in 2003 resurfaced, bringing back the joy and excitement I felt stepping off the plane for the first time. That fearless Gatinha, who was never afraid of anything or anyone and knew she had a brilliant future ahead, was back. The overwhelming sense of self-love and fulfilment made me want to hug the nearest person and share my happiness. I felt God was finally pleased with me, as I could now see the lights He had been trying to show me through friends and family—lights I had been too blind to notice before.

The flight to Barcelona was uneventful, but the city greeted me with its vibrant and captivating energy. I wandered through its narrow streets, the cobblestones beneath my feet echoing with history. The sounds of street musicians playing lively tunes, the aroma of fresh paella wafting through the air, and the colourful mosaic tiles of Park Güell dazzled my eyes. I let the beauty of the city envelop me, distracting me from any lingering doubts.

Barcelona's charm seeped into my soul, and I soaked in the culture with every step. The warmth of the sun on my skin, the distant sound of waves crashing against the shore, and the laughter of locals and tourists alike filled me with a sense of belonging and excitement. I visited the majestic Sagrada Familia, its intricate details and towering spires a testament to human creativity and perseverance. I strolled down La Rambla, absorbing the lively atmosphere and vibrant street life. The market stalls, bursting with fresh produce and artisanal goods, added a sensory feast to my experience.

Each moment in Barcelona was a celebration of life, the companion of Sandra who happily guided me around her hometown. I felt more alive than I had in the last few years, free from the chains that were holding me back. The city's energy mirrored my own renewed spirit, and I embraced every experience with open arms. The vibrant colours, the rich textures, and the melodic sounds of the city became a backdrop to my personal renaissance. As I explored the city, I knew that this trip was not just a getaway, but a journey back to myself—a rediscovery of the Gatinha who was fearless, adventurous, and ready to embrace the future with a full heart.

Chapter 10
Messages from the Heart

Saturday morning, I awoke to a room so dark that I could hardly make out the shapes around me. The blackness was almost tangible, like a velvet curtain pulled tight around my senses. My eyes strained to adjust, but it was the soft, persistent vibration that had stirred me from my sleep—a low hum reverberating through the walls. It was as if some unseen machine had sprung to life in the early hours, its mechanical heart beating in tandem with mine. I lay still for a moment, my mind sluggishly trying to pinpoint the source. Perhaps it was the Wi-Fi box, tucked away in its corner, or maybe the familiar hum of the refrigerator in the kitchen, an old friend whose steady noise often lulled me into a false sense of security.

As I pondered the origins of the sound, I mumbled a groggy command to Alexa, asking for the time. Her voice cut through the darkness with crisp clarity: "5 a.m." Though I had been awake for what felt like an eternity, I knew I couldn't stay in bed any longer. I threw back the covers and made my way to the bathroom, the cool morning air nipping at my skin.

Stepping into the shower, I was greeted by the bracing shock of cold water—a ritual I had come to cherish since the day I surrendered to God. The cold was a jolt to my system, a cleansing that reached beyond the physical. It felt like a baptism, the icy water washing away not just the sweat and grime of the night but also the doubts and fears that clung to my soul. As the water cascaded over me, I lathered my body with soap, the rich, intoxicating scent of roses and almonds filling the steamy air. The fragrance was divine, a luxurious blend that softened my skin to a silken sheen. It was more than just a bath; it was a sensory experience that soothed my mind and spirit—a brief escape from the thoughts that constantly swirled in my head.

The sound of water splashing against the tiles was a comforting rhythm, a steady beat that allowed my mind to wander. It had been a week since I last heard from Gato, a week of silence that gnawed at the edges of my thoughts. As I closed my eyes, the image of his face came unbidden to my mind—his cat-eyes, the curve of his lips, the warmth of his gentle smile. I found myself questioning if it had all been a dream, a figment of my imagination conjured by a longing heart. The memory of our encounter at the bus stop surfaced, the way my heart had skipped a beat when the thought of him being "the one" had crossed my mind.

But as I turned off the shower and wrapped myself in a towel, doubts began to creep in. Perhaps he had only been bored that day, looking for a fleeting distraction, and now that I had gone to Barcelona, his interest had faded like a wisp of smoke. Or maybe, a more unsettling thought whispered, he had a girlfriend all along. I forced myself to silence these thoughts, pushing them down into the depths of my consciousness. My inner voice, that instinctual whisper that came from somewhere deep within, urged me to reach out to him. The command was clear, echoing in the quiet of my mind—text him. I decided that I would, later in the afternoon, ask if he was still up for that coffee.

With a renewed sense of purpose, I dressed quickly and headed to the gym, determined to make the most of my free time away from my studies and the tumultuous process of changing careers. The weights clanked in the gym, and the rhythmic thud of my feet on the treadmill was a welcome distraction from the uncertainty that gnawed at me.

By the time afternoon rolled around, the sun was high, casting a warm glow through the windows. Around 3 p.m., I finally picked up my phone, my fingers hovering over the screen as I searched for Gato's name in my contacts. I remembered how I had deleted all our previous chats, a futile attempt to move on after he hadn't texted back since I left for Barcelona. Yet here I was, typing out a message: "Hi, neighbour. How are you? If you're not busy tomorrow, and feel free to say no, would you have time for that coffee?"

I hit send and stared at the screen, my heart pounding in my chest. His reply was almost immediate, my phone vibrating with his message. He greeted me politely, but then explained that he was out of town and couldn't meet up. My heart sank a little as I read his words, unsure of how to respond. I hesitated, my mind racing with what to type next, when another message from him popped up: "Could you do Tuesday?"

Relief washed over me, and I quickly typed back: "Yes. That would be great."

Our conversation ended there, brief and to the point, and yet I didn't feel the excitement I had expected. I decided then not to dwell on it, to push thoughts of Gato to the back of my mind until the day we would finally meet. There was no sense in overthinking it now. Instead, I focused on the rest of my day, determined to enjoy my weekend and the freedom it offered.

Chapter 11
Fading Connections

It was a humid Tuesday afternoon, the kind where the warmth lingered in the air, clinging lightly to your skin but never quite stifling. My small apartment maintained a pleasant, steady temperature, the thick walls offering a natural barrier against the summer heat. Outside, the world was unusually quiet, save for the occasional chirps of birds that seemed to carry a melody of their own. My flat faced the back of another building, isolating me from the distant sounds of traffic and city life, enveloping me instead in the soft, soothing whispers of nature, which occasionally broke the stillness with a rustle or a flutter.

I was lost in my thoughts, reflecting on the complexities of my life and the peculiar twists that had brought me here, when my phone, lying unnoticed on the table, buzzed sharply. The vibration sliced through the silence, jolting me from my reverie.

Glancing at the screen, I expected nothing more than a routine notification—a reminder, perhaps, or an unimportant message. But then his name flashed across the display—Gato. My heart skipped a beat, a reflexive response that surprised me. The excitement I once felt at seeing his name was now replaced by a dull ache of anticipation mingled with disappointment. I opened the message, my breath hitching slightly in my throat. His words were brief, a few lines at most, and the familiar rhythm of his writing felt like an echo of the connection we once shared.

He explained how his Tuesday had filled up unexpectedly, how he couldn't make it as we'd planned. There was an apology hidden within his words, but it was faint, almost an afterthought—more a formality than a genuine expression of regret. Reading his message felt like watching a once vibrant painting fade into muted hues; the colours of our connection, once bright and vivid, were now slipping away into obscurity.

My interest in Gato had been waning, a slow and steady decline like the final embers of a fire fading into cold ash. Each unreturned message and postponed meeting had chipped away at the enthusiasm I once felt. His message did nothing to revive the dying flame; if anything, it extinguished it further. I responded with as much emotion as I could muster—which, admittedly, wasn't much. My words were dry, deliberately chosen to reflect the disinterest that had started to take root in me. I typed out a polite reply, masking the disillusionment that had settled in my chest.

He suggested we meet on Thursday or perhaps over the weekend, trying to salvage what little remained of our connection. I felt a twinge of something—was it hope? Regret? It was hard to tell. After a brief hesitation, I agreed to Thursday. Thc wcckcnd fclt too distant, too uncertain, and perhaps a part of me wanted to give this one last try—a final chance to see if there was anything left worth holding onto. But deep down, I knew that I was only prolonging the inevitable.

As I set my phone down, the room seemed to close in around me. The soft chirps of the birds outside felt muted now, almost mocking, as I reflected on how quickly things had changed. I sank back into my thoughts, the warmth of the afternoon sun filtering through the window, reminding me of the warmth I had once felt when thinking about Gato. I wondered if I was chasing a memory rather than a reality, clinging to the hope that something—anything—could reignite that spark.

Chapter 12
First Date: Steels Pub

Thursday morning dawned with a different energy, a sense of lightness and anticipation that filled the air. My mum had flown in from Brazil, bringing with her a burst of joy and warmth that immediately spread throughout my home. Her laughter, bright and infectious, echoed through the rooms, making everything seem a little more vibrant. We decided on a whim, to make lunch together, a simple idea that quickly turned into something more, a spontaneous family gathering that felt like a reunion. The kitchen was a hive of activity, the comforting smell of roast chicken mingling with the fresh, earthy scent of herbs and spices. Brazilian music played softly from the speakers, adding a lively, rhythmic backdrop to the scene.

As I prepared lunch, my mum chatted animatedly on the phone with my sister, as it was my niece's 3rd birthday, her voice full of life as they exchanged the latest gossip and planning the weekend party. It was a scene that brought back memories of my childhood, filling me with a deep sense of nostalgia and contentment. Cooking had always been my way of expressing love, a passion I had cultivated during the years I spent living alone. Over time, though, that passion had waned, buried under the demands and distractions of daily life. But today, with my family around me, it felt like that old spark was being reignited, the flames of joy and connection fuelling it back to life.

The timer on the oven beeped, pulling me from my thoughts. I turned to check on the chicken, its golden skin crackling as it released a rich, savoury aroma. The scent took me back to family dinners from my teenage years, when food was more than just sustenance, it was the centrepiece of our gatherings, a way to show love without words. My mum's laughter drew me back to the present, and she called out that my phone was ringing. Without hesitation, I wiped my hands on a dish towel and took the phone from her, smiling as she continued to chat and laugh on the phone.

It was Gato again. A flicker of something—perhaps anticipation—stirred within me when I saw his name on the screen. He asked if I could meet him that afternoon, suggesting we grab a coffee. There was a casualness to his message, ending with a kiss that felt more like an afterthought than a sincere gesture. I replied simply, "I will be in free after 4 p.m." His response was quick, "Okay great," but I couldn't tell if he was actually pleased or just going through the motions. I let him know I'd be home, and he could text me when he was ready to meet. The conversation ended as quickly as it had begun, leaving me glancing at the clock, realising it was almost time to go.

At 4.01 p.m., another message from Gato. He asked if 4.30 p.m. was too soon, and since I was already dressed and ready, I agreed. I was wearing black leggings, a short grey jumper with a hood, and my trainers, a casual outfit that matched the informality of our planned meeting. He sent the name of the place: The Steels Pub on Haverstock Hill. A pub, I thought. My hope that Gato might be the one, might share my preference for a life without alcohol, was slowly fading. But I pushed the thought aside, reminding myself that this was about giving us a final chance.

As I stood in front of the mirror, I debated whether to put on makeup. In the end, I decided against it. I wanted him to see me again as I was, without the mask that foundation and concealer could provide. My eyelashes were already done, adding a touch of glamour, and I had just finished doing my hair. I parted it down the middle, letting my straight black hair frame my face. There was something about the way it looked that reminded me of my Greek heritage, a reflection of my father's side of the family. I spritzed on my favourite perfume, a scent that always made me feel confident, and with a final glance in the mirror, I was ready.

The journey to the pub was filled with a swirl of emotions: anticipation, doubt, and a surprising sense of calm. As I stepped out of my apartment, the sounds of the city were replaced by the quiet rustle of leaves and the soft chirping of birds. The distant honk of a car horn was barely audible, the rhythmic click of my trainers against the pavement providing a steady beat to the soundtrack of my thoughts. The air was slight cold, carrying the faint scent of blooming flowers, mixed with the earthy smell of the city.

As I approached the pub, the gate was already open, giving me a clear view of the interior. There he was, standing at the threshold, half-inside and half-out, as if he couldn't decide whether to stay or go. He was anxiously shifting his weight, clearly trying to spot me. My heart seemed to leap into my throat, pounding so hard that I felt like I was wearing it on my sleeve. The closer I got, the more I wondered how I was even managing to walk—my legs felt like they could give out at any moment. All I could see were his cat-like eyes locked onto mine, piercing through me as though he could see right into my soul.

I could barely manage a simple "Hi" as I neared him. The sight of him left me breathless, shocked by how strikingly handsome he was. This was not the same man I had briefly met at the bus stop; this version of Gato was polished, magnetic. But those eyes, his warm smile, those were the same. We exchanged a quick kiss on the cheek, a polite greeting, but I couldn't stop staring at him.

He was wearing a pair of well-fitted jeans, crisp white sneakers, and a slim, white shirt that contrasted beautifully against his strong chest and shoulders, which was visible and impossible not to notice, over a grey, woolly jumper—a look that reminded me of the prototypical English gentleman, straight out of a movie. He looked absolutely gorgeous, and the more he gazed at me, the more my heart pounded in my chest. A warmth began to rise within me, not from the weather, but from his mere presence.

As he led me inside to the bar, I tried to gather my thoughts, but it was difficult to focus with him so close. We exchanged a few words, but it felt like the entire world had narrowed down to just him and me. I could barely make out the blonde bartender behind the counter, waiting for us to order. Gato asked me what I'd like, and without really thinking, I blurted out *"a gin and tonic,"* even though it wasn't my favourite drink at all. I was minding my training and diet, avoiding alcohol to prioritise my health, but I ordered it anyway, knowing I wouldn't drink much.

As Gato leant forward to place his order, his eyes scanned the bottles lined up behind the bar, searching intently for something specific. His movements were deliberate, confident, yet casual, and I found myself captivated by the way he carried himself. Then, in that smooth, sexy British accent that sent a shiver down my spine, he calmly asked for a soft drink or sparkling water. And in that precise moment, I went on silent mode, it was as if the entire universe had unfolded before my very eyes, expanding with an overwhelming force of clarity and realisation. The pub, bustling just a second ago, seemed to fall eerily silent, and time itself slowed to a near halt.

It felt like the beginning of creation, like I was witnessing my own personal Big Bang, the very genesis of something monumental and life-altering. The air around us seemed to crackle with energy, as though we were standing at the epicentre of an explosion, where everything that had been waiting to come into existence was finally bursting forth. The ground beneath my feet trembled slightly, as if in response to this cosmic revelation, while vibrant, colourful lights began to dance before my eyes, like the scattered remnants of stars being born.

In that fleeting moment, we were the very centre of the universe, the point from which all things emerged and expanded. My heart pounded in my chest, matching the rhythm of this newly created world. My inner voice spoke with a clarity and certainty that left no room for doubt. It's him. The words echoed through me, reverberating with the force of truth. My mind, once clouded by uncertainty, now echoed the same sentiment, louder, more insistent. "He's the one."

I was enveloped by a profound sense of connection, as if the entirety of existence had conspired to bring us to this very moment. Everything else faded away—the dim lights of the pub, the murmurs of other patrons, the clinking of glasses—leaving just the two of us in the centre of this cosmic dance. The universe itself seemed to acknowledge the significance of this encounter, as if it had been waiting for this moment all along.

I struggled to keep my composure, to focus on the present moment as I watched him. He turned to pay, and his eyes met mine again. A fire blazed within me, igniting my entire body. As we walked towards a corner table, I couldn't even feel the floor beneath my feet. All I could see was this stunning man, this unexpected gift who had walked into my life.

We sat down, and the conversation began to flow effortlessly, as if we had known each other for ages. There were no awkward silences, just a natural rhythm between us. Despite the heat building in my body, I couldn't take off my jumper; underneath, I was wearing only my gym bra, and I didn't want my chest to be a distraction. My boobs, already on the larger side, would have been hard to ignore in such a setting. Feeling the intensity of the moment, I asked if we could move outside. Without hesitation, Gato agreed, and we found a spot outdoors.

As we walked outside, I was only vaguely aware of the other people around us. My entire focus was on him, his charming personality, his enthusiasm as he talked about his job and life. He explained how busy his schedule was, making sure to emphasise that his biggest challenge was finding time off. It felt like an explanation for why it had taken us two weeks to finally meet, but I didn't mind. I believed in the timing of things, and it seemed that now was the perfect moment for us.

As I shared parts of my story, I noticed the way he looked at me, with warmth and genuine care. His eyes held a sweetness and peacefulness that I hadn't seen before. It was hard to tear my gaze away from him, especially with his lips partially hidden by a neatly trimmed beard. As we talked, we realised how much we already had in common—our passion for fitness and nutrition, our similar lifestyles.

Then he asked me where I live in Hampstead, and I answered, "At Holly Hill." There was a moment of silence, and then I repeated it a couple more times, thinking he did not understand. I then asked, "Did you understand what I said?" He looked surprised and shocked, with something in his eyes that indicated disbelief, and he replied, "I live in Holly Hill also." The coincidence amused me—he lives at number 2, and I live at number 8, yet we had never crossed paths in the year I had been in the area. It was clear that the universe, on that morning, was conspiring for us to finally meet.

I knew the reason why that happened—because I asked God for him, and I was ready to receive it. God had sent me my perfect match in less than 72 hours, and I couldn't believe how seamlessly Gato fit into the picture.

Of course, I knew I still had to see if he possessed the other values I had prayed for. But at that moment, I was in awe of how God had not only heard my prayers but had answered them with even more than I had asked for. There Gato was, a gorgeous English gentleman, and I couldn't help but feel that he was my gift from above. After spending a couple delightful hours together, it was time to part ways. Gato had a meeting to attend, and as we left the cosy pub, the late afternoon sunbathed everything in a golden light. We had been seated outside, where the warmth of the day lingered in the air, mingling with the scents of fresh grass and the occasional aroma of nearby food vendors.

As we walked side by side, our footsteps created a rhythmic accompaniment to our easy conversation. We laughed about how Gato had been right at the bus stop when he had confidently remarked that he looked better than he did that day. He even joked that his appearance was not yet "upper level," implying that his true self was yet to be fully revealed. His laughter was infectious, amplifying the warmth of the day and making our time together even more enjoyable.

Approaching the traffic light, the air was filled with the comforting warmth of late summer and the occasional fragrance of leaves from the trees. As we stood by the crossing signal, the bright colours of the traffic lights flickered, casting a cheerful glow over us.

Our goodbye was casual yet sincere. We didn't make any concrete plans for the future, simply expressing how glad we were to have shared this pleasant afternoon. Gato made a left turn, heading in a different direction, and as I waited for the light to change, I turned to look back at him. He stood a short distance away, staring at me, his face bathed in the soft afternoon light. His smile was warm and genuine, and his eyes conveyed a sweet, caring look that seemed to mirror my own feelings.

I smiled back, my heart still fluttering with the warmth of our encounter. As the traffic light turned green and the crosswalk signal blinked to life, I waved to him one last time, I turned and walked towards my flat, carrying with me the lingering warmth of our time together and the hopeful anticipation of what might come next.

There I was, walking in quiet self-reflection, still trying to wrap my mind around everything that had happened in the last few days. Three days ago, I had found myself in a deep conversation with God, pouring out my soul, seeking answer to my question that had weighed heavily on my heart. Incredibly, within just 30 minutes of that conversation, I had received the clarity I was searching for—the answer to my question that had come with such speed and certainty that I was left in awe.

And now, less than 72 hours later, another revelation had fallen into place. This time, it wasn't just an answer, but the fulfilment of the wish—Gato. I couldn't help but wonder at the timing of it all. It seemed too perfect to be mere coincidence. Just days after my conversation with God, here he was, walking into my life—something out of a dream. How could I doubt it? Everything about him, his lifestyle, his interests, even his life story, mirrored mine in such remarkable ways. It was as if the universe had arranged for our paths to cross at precisely the right moment.

We were both wanderers at heart, leaving home young to chase dreams we couldn't ignore. The familiar pull of wanting more, of stepping into the unknown, was something we both understood intimately. But it was more than just shared ambition. Gato had built his life in nutrition—the exact career I had dreamt of when I was a teenager. I could still remember the passion, the excitement, the certainty I had felt about becoming a part of that world. I was so close to diving into it, ready to make that dream my reality.

But then God had nudged me in a different direction, one I hadn't seen coming. Instead of staying on that path, I felt called to something greater. I was meant to cross oceans, to leave behind the life I had imagined for something even bigger. At the time, I didn't understand it fully, but I knew it wasn't just about me. It was about my family, about changing the course of our lives in ways I couldn't yet see.

But still, the questions lingered. *Was this all part of a divine plan, or was I simply seeing what I wanted to see? Could Gato truly be the one I had been waiting for? Or was there more to this than I could yet understand?*

Yet now, standing here in this moment, it was impossible to ignore the strange, almost eerie parallels between Gato's life and the life I had once envisioned for myself. The man I had wished for—he seemed to be standing right in front of me. *How could I doubt that he was the one when everything lined up so perfectly?* The synchronicities felt too strong to dismiss, as if every step I had taken, every decision I had made, had led me to this very moment.

I walked on, my mind racing with possibilities. The air around me was crisp, the sky darkening as the day drew to a close, but inside, I felt the quiet stir of something unfolding. I wasn't sure what the future held, and I didn't need to know just yet. All I knew was that I had asked for answers and a wish to be granted, and within less than 72 hours, life had brought Gato into my life. I was unsure of the significance of this event and why it was him and why I was involved in his life. Despite these uncertainties, I accepted it, I was eager to uncover the answers, and my curiosity drove me to ask questions. But I was ready to find out.

As I opened the door to my flat, a soft buzz from my phone interrupted the quiet. A message. I wasn't expecting it so soon—barely three hours had passed since I'd met Gato. Yet, there he was, already on my screen, his words conveying how much he enjoyed meeting me.

I smiled, replying in agreement, my fingers pausing briefly over the screen as I added a playful comment about how surprised I was that afternoon. He caught on right away, sending a string of laugh emojis, telling me he'd taken it as a compliment. And it was. He was handsome, undeniably sexy, and his confidence was magnetic.

There was something about his straightforwardness that struck a chord in me. No games, no dancing around intentions—just direct, honest communication. He wasn't one to waste time. That's what I found irresistible in that man.

Without hesitation, he suggested we meet again. My answer was an easy "yes." From there, we exchanged a few flirtatious messages, each of us dancing around how impressed we had been by the other's looks, though neither of us could hide the underlying wow that we both felt. The physical attraction was undeniable, but there was more to it—something deeper, something electric. And we both knew it.

Then, in that confident, gentlemanly way that I was already beginning to admire, he asked if I'd have dinner with him the next evening. The way he phrased it, so polite yet so certain, made it impossible to say anything but "definitely, yes." And just like that, he took the reins. Gato didn't hesitate; he planned the entire evening, right down to the time he'd pick me up.

For once, I didn't have to lift a finger. It was like a scene straight out of a movie. Usually, I was the one deciding, planning for others, organising every little detail. But here was a man I barely knew, taking care of everything as if he had known me forever, as if he understood what I needed without a word.

Maybe it was old-fashioned of me, but I liked it—being led, allowing someone else to take control. All I had to do was look my best, to step into a higher version of myself, the version that I felt he deserved. The excitement coursing through me was undeniable. There was something different about this. Something exhilarating. I could already feel it: the promise of something incredible lingering in the air, just waiting for tomorrow.

Chapter 13
First Dinner

What a beautiful way to wake up. The first thing I felt was a wave of gratitude for opening my eyes to this special day ahead. I stretched, savouring the calmness of the morning, then rolled out of bed and headed toward the shower. My morning routine, but today felt different. There was an unusual silence in the air, almost as if the world outside had paused just for me. I couldn't hear anything but the music inside my head. A melody, soft and persistent, with a name—Gato. I chuckled to myself, the cold water cascading down my skin, its sharp bite jolting me awake. God, I had forgotten how refreshing it was to wake up feeling light, unburdened, my eyes bright and alive. Every touch against my skin felt new, like I was rediscovering myself.

After my shower, I reached for one of my favourite body lotions, a gift from my mother, thoughtfully brought from home. The scent, a mix of ripe passionfruit and Brazilian nuts, instantly transported me back to my hometown. The memories came flooding in—the sun-kissed days, the laughter, and the warmth of familiar faces. I massaged the lotion into my skin, the coolness of the cream leaving a silky softness behind, a luxurious reminder of home and all the love that came with it.

Without any need to rush, I took my time. I brewed a cup of coffee, black and strong as my hair, letting the rich aroma fill the room as I made my way to the window. A mix of sun and grey sky, and still, it felt like a canvas for my thoughts. I savoured each sip of my black coffee, its smooth bitterness balanced by the subtle hint of vanilla. My mind wandered playfully, and I found myself wondering, with a quiet smirk, *Would Gato be a vanilla type of person?* "Well, I am a vanilla myself," I answer my own question. The thought made me laugh out loud, the sound bright and carefree in the quiet room. There was something contagious about my mood—light, joyful, and completely in tune with myself.

Shaking my head, I set the coffee cup down, amused at my silly thoughts. Tonight was going to be just a simple dinner. Dinner for two. Yet, the mere thought of being near Gato had my pulse quickening, my mind racing with anticipation. How was I possibly going to keep myself from kissing those lips, lips I couldn't seem to stop staring at in my mind? I closed my eyes, trying to ground myself, to bring my thoughts back to reality, but the flutter in my stomach refused to settle.

I took a deep breath, reminding myself of the tasks at hand. A workout awaited me, and some pampering was in order before the evening. Yes, I thought with a smile, it's officially a date. But the strangest part? Again, there was no tension, no nervous flutter of anxiety. Instead, I felt calm, confident, and completely at ease with the idea of tonight. The thought of seeing Gato stirred something inside me—something exciting, yet peaceful. I wasn't worried about the night ahead; I was ready to embrace it.

As I stood there, gazing out at the open sky, I could feel the day unfolding before me, full of promise and possibility. I wasn't just preparing for a date; I was preparing for a moment. A moment where everything felt aligned, where I could simply be, without fear or hesitation. And as the energy in the room seemed to pulse with my excitement, I realised that tonight could be the beginning of something beautiful. Something I was more than ready for, "Was I?"

I played one of my favourite rock bands as I got ready for the night ahead. Their familiar melodies filled the room, soft yet powerful, each note weaving effortlessly into the rhythm of my movements. The music pulsed through the space, every beat syncing with the flutter of my heartbeat, and as I brushed my hair, I savoured the feel of the smooth strands beneath my fingertips. It was as though each stroke of the brush aligned with the comforting hum of the guitar riffs, grounding me, yet at the same time infusing me with a spark of energy and anticipation.

This was more than just getting ready for a night out—it was a ritual, a moment of self-care, of embracing my own presence before stepping into the world. The music gave me life, a soundtrack to the unspoken dialogue between my thoughts and my reflections. I smiled at myself in the mirror, feeling the power of this moment. Tonight, I decided, why not go all out? A date like this deserved it. No, I deserved it.

After all, this wasn't just any date—it was with Gato. There was something about him that made everything feel elevated, like the universe had finally aligned in my favour. I didn't even think it was possible to ask for someone like him, but God, it seemed, had other plans. I had never expected someone who wasn't just good-looking but so much more—kind, intelligent, magnetic. I didn't want to believe that such a combination existed in one person, that it was even possible to ask for so much. But here he was, a gift from Heaven.

God, in all His infinite wisdom, had sent Gato into my life, showing me that nothing was too much, that perhaps it wasn't about asking for less but allowing myself to believe I was deserving of more. More than I had ever thought possible. The truth was, we often limit ourselves, believing that too much is too much, that wanting more is unreasonable. But tonight, in this moment, I began to realise something profound—I deserved it all. Every bit of it. More than I had dared to imagine.

And as the music swelled around me, I embraced that thought, allowing it to fill me with confidence. I was ready—not just for tonight, but for all the beautiful things that were yet to come.

As I moved to the vanity, I carefully applied my makeup. I wanted my eyes to shine tonight, to glow with a brightness he couldn't ignore. I blended shades of rich brown eyeshadow into the crease, adding a subtle shimmer to the lids that caught the light just right, making my brown eyes sparkle with an almost mischievous glint. I loved the way the soft, golden flecks danced every time I blinked, like they were holding a secret only he was meant to uncover. Tonight, everything had to speak—my eyes, my lips, my skin.

My hair, sleek and black, fell effortlessly over my shoulders. I styled my bangs to frame my face gently, sweeping them to the sides for a softer, sweeter look. It felt right—tonight, I wanted to exude warmth and sweetness, to reflect exactly how I felt inside. My excitement felt almost tangible, like the static before a summer storm.

The dress I chose was perfect—black, with a short, cinched waist that accentuated my figure, and a skirt that flared out in a delicate, round shape, reminiscent of a ballerina's tutu. It had just the right amount of movement, swaying gently with every step I took, making me feel both graceful and free. The way the fabric floated around my thighs gave the dress an almost ethereal quality, as if I could twirl and dance at any moment. It was the kind of dress that made me feel like I was on stage, poised and ready for the spotlight, but with a softness that hinted at the sweetness I wanted to exude tonight.

The waist, tightly gathered, hugged me just enough to define my silhouette, while the skirt cascaded down, flowing effortlessly over my hips. I loved how it moved with me, brushing against my tanned legs, making me feel delicate yet powerful at the same time.

As I stood in front of the mirror, I couldn't help but smile at how the dress complemented every detail of the night I was about to step into. It was playful, feminine, and a little mysterious—just like how I felt inside. And tonight, it would tell a story, just like everything else: the perfume, the makeup, the hair. I wanted Gato to see me, all of me, from the sparkle in my eyes to the sway of my skirt. I was ready for this moment, and I was ready for him.

As I glanced in the mirror, I couldn't help but notice the way my chest gleamed under the soft glow of the lights. The delicate fabric of my dress hugged my curves in just the right way, highlighting my full, firm breasts, creating a silhouette that was impossible to ignore. I didn't try to hide them—why should I? I loved the way I looked tonight, and there was something empowering about owning my body and how it moved beneath the dress. A brief, playful thought crossed my mind: *What if I didn't wear knickers tonight?* The idea of feeling that free, embracing the night with a hint of rebellion, lingered for a moment before reality tugged me back. I chuckled to myself, amused at the naughty thought. Maybe not just yet. After all, I didn't want to scare Gato away before we even began.

But it wasn't fear of rejection that made me laugh. It was the thrilling sense that I could push the boundaries, knowing that Gato wasn't the kind of man to be easily rattled. There was something about him—a calm, steady presence that seemed more than capable of handling everything I brought with me, both physically and emotionally. Gato wasn't just handsome; he exuded a quiet confidence that spoke volumes. He was the type of man who didn't need to announce his strength or capability—it was simply there, radiating from him with every step, every glance.

And tonight, I was ready to meet him, as the Brazilian girl who stood proudly and unapologetically in her own skin. A woman who knew exactly what she was bringing to the table—passion, complexity, sensuality—and someone who didn't want any longer to settle for less than she deserved. Gato, with his charm and self-assuredness, seemed like the man who could embrace all of that, who wouldn't shy away from the intensity of who I was. And that thought made me feel even more alive.

As I waited for the clock to turn to 9.15 p.m., the excitement built in my chest, buzzing like electricity. Every minute felt heavier with anticipation, my senses heightened. The scent of my Tom Ford Lost Cherry perfume lingered in the air, sweet and intoxicating, filling the room with a warmth that seemed almost visible, as though the fragrance had a life of its own. It was one of my favourite scents—rich with cherries, a touch of almond, and a deep, velvety base that felt as luxurious as it smelled. It was a scent you could almost see, like a ribbon of crimson weaving through the air, pulling you closer.

Then, at 9.12 p.m., my phone buzzed. Right on time. I smiled to myself—Gato never disappointed. Is he like me, respecting time and people? A trait I deeply appreciated. I was a punctual person, and it was rare to find someone who mirrored that. But there he was, his message lighting up my phone three minutes before our agreed time. It said something about him—that he valued this moment, just as I did.

I took one last look at myself in the mirror, feeling the butterflies in my stomach awaken, their wings brushing against the inside of my chest. The night ahead was full of promise, and I was ready for it. My heart raced with excitement, the anticipation of what was to come lingering in the air, as tangible as the scent of my perfume. Tonight, I was stepping into something new, and with Gato's message still glowing on my screen, I knew I was ready for whatever this evening had in store.

There I go, running down the staircase, the clack of my heels echoing with each step, though they weren't too high—I wanted to be quick. I couldn't wait any longer to see him. My heart raced, not just from the pace but from the anticipation of what was waiting for me outside. As I reached the pavement, there he was, standing outside the taxi with the door already open, as if he'd been waiting for this moment as eagerly as I had.

He looked absolutely stunning. A dark tweed blazer draped effortlessly over a slim-fitting crew neck jumper, the colours blending perfectly in a way that felt both casual and impossibly elegant. The cool evening air swirled around us, but all I could focus on was him. There was something magnetic about the way he stood there, eyes fixed on me as though nothing else in the world existed. He looked both confident and a little stunned, as if the sight of me had frozen him in place. His eyes, bright and shining, cat-like in their intensity, seemed to speak volumes, even though his lips hadn't yet formed a word.

As I approached, I felt a sudden urge to twirl, to give him the full effect of the dress. So I did, spinning around playfully, letting the skirt of my ballerina-like dress float out around me. His eyes followed every movement, a mix of admiration and disbelief washing over his face. When I finally locked eyes with him again, I smiled, letting the playful energy between us build, and whispered, "Welcome to Brazil."

His face softened, his smile spreading, but it wasn't just his lips that smiled—it was his entire face. His eyes, still wide with awe, twinkled as if they were laughing along with me, completely lost for words. I could tell in that moment that I'd done it. I'd made the impression I wanted. My mission was complete.

He stepped forward, still holding the door for me like the gentleman he was, his hand brushing mine as I climbed into the car. My heart raced again, not from the chill of the night, but from the excitement coursing through me. I settled into the seat, a mix of nerves and giddy energy bubbling up inside me. As he slid in beside me, smooth and effortless like a cat, I couldn't help but remember the first time I saw him—his eyes, the same cat-like gaze, jumping in front of me at the bus stop. It felt like déjà vu, yet so much more intimate now.

He couldn't stop staring at me, those eyes locking onto mine, and when he finally spoke, his voice was soft but full of admiration. "You look beautiful." His words, so simple, melted my heart. How could someone make me feel so powerful, so confident, just by looking at me? It was as if his gaze alone wrapped me in this bubble of invincibility, and in that moment, I felt like nothing could touch me.

As the driver headed toward a bar restaurant in Camden Town, the quiet hum of the car's engine filled the space between us. Gato had chosen to keep things local, and I loved that. Camden had a vibrancy, an edge that made every street feel alive, and I knew the night ahead would be nothing short of magical. We chatted during the ride, though I struggled to stay focused. My thoughts kept drifting to what it would be like to kiss him, to feel his arms around me. There was this tension between us—not uncomfortable, but a kind of careful restraint. He was being a perfect gentleman, not crossing any lines, but I could feel the pull. It was there, electric in the space between our bodies.

The night outside was cooler than I'd expected, a crispness in the air that hinted at the changing seasons. The city lights blurred as we sped through the streets, a mixture of colours reflecting on the windows, but all I could think about was him.

When we arrived at the restaurant, his excitement was palpable. He turned to me, his eyes sparkling, and asked me to wait while he got out to open the car door for me. I laughed to myself, amazed by his chivalry. "I've never had that before," I thought. "But I could get used to it." The door opened, and I stepped out into the cool night air. The sound of music and laughter floated from the club ahead, mixing with the distant hum of the city. Camden was alive, the streets buzzing with energy, but all I felt was the heat between us.

As we began walking toward the entrance, I didn't even think—I just reached for his hand. It felt like the most natural thing in the world, and the moment my fingers intertwined with his, a wave of warmth rushed through me. His hand was firm but gentle, like he'd been waiting for this touch as long as I had. It was the smallest of gestures, but in that instant, it felt like the universe had aligned just for us. It wasn't just a date—it was a gift. A gift from the universe, from God, from something far bigger than either of us.

As we walked, I could feel the present moment wrapping itself around me like a warm blanket. I let go of everything else—the past, the future. Right now, all that mattered was this. Him, me, and the night ahead. I smiled, silently grateful for the months I had spent learning about Stoicism, about living in the now. This was what it meant to truly be in the present, and I wasn't about to let a single moment slip away.

We stepped up to the doors, the night just beginning, and I knew, deep down, that whatever happened next would be unforgettable.

Chapter 14
Dinner Time

As we passed through the entrance, bypassing the crowd and heading directly to the reception, I felt an overwhelming sense of anticipation. The place was alive with energy. Inside, the dim lighting cast a soft, red glow across the space, highlighting the sensual artwork on the walls—bold, rich paintings that oozed with passion. The whole atmosphere seemed to synchronise perfectly with the fire building inside me. Everything felt heightened: the sounds of conversation, the faint murmur of music in the background. It was as if the place itself was pulsating with the same electricity that was coursing through me.

When we arrived at our table, I noticed how quickly Gato assessed the seating arrangement. His attention to detail, always so precise. As I took my seat, facing the restaurant, he leant in close, his voice soft but deliberate, asking, "Do you mind if I sit right next to you?" Oh God, he couldn't have asked a better question if he tried. My heart leaped, and without hesitation, I practically squealed, "Yes, of course!"

I slid to the right, squeezing myself to the edge of the seat, nearly perching on the armrest just to be closer to him. I didn't care about space—I only wanted to feel him next to me. The warmth of his body was intoxicating. I couldn't stop smiling, feeling giddy like a child handed their favourite ice cream on a hot summer day. Every time I glanced at him, I caught his eyes lingering on me, and I could see in them the same unspoken thoughts that were racing through my own mind—wondering what his kiss would feel like, what it would be like to be wrapped in his arms. His presence made me dream, even as I sat wide awake.

As we looked over the menu, we both tried to focus on the words in front of us, when it came time to order, he took the lead effortlessly, yet with a quiet grace that made it clear he was thinking of me. His voice was steady, but before he made any decision, he always paused, turning to ask if I liked this or that, his eyes scanning my face for approval. The way he cared, how he ensured I would enjoy every bite, made me feel cherished, like the luckiest woman in the world.

There was something undeniably comforting in his attentiveness. He wasn't just focused on what we were ordering—he was focused on me. Every detail, every small gesture, showed that he was attuned to my comfort, my happiness. And as he finalised the choices, I couldn't help but smile, feeling like I was exactly where I was meant to be, in the company of a man who saw me, who wanted me to feel not just content, but special.

We spoke about life, about the things we wanted in a partner, and with each topic, it became clearer that this wasn't just a fleeting connection—it was something deeper. Every box was being checked, effortlessly. The ease of our conversation, the way time slipped away without us noticing, felt almost unreal. It was as if I'd known him from another life, as though our souls had met long before this night. In that moment, I believed in the impossible, because everything about him, about us, felt possible.

His voice was like a melody, each word sinking into my mind, swirling around in my brain. I could feel my blood rush with every syllable he spoke. His deep, rich tone reverberated through me, and I could physically feel it—like his voice was writing itself into my skin. My body grew warmer, and I had to pull my hair up, the heat creeping up my neck. I caught his gaze as I tied my hair, his eyes following every movement, captivated by even the simplest of actions.

Then the food arrived. The scent of freshly grilled chicken and lamb chops filled the air, a mix of savoury and rich aromas that made my stomach rumble in delight. There were fries—because, of course, it was a night out—and fresh, warm bread, the kind that makes you close your eyes and breathe in the comforting, familiar smell. I loved bread, and as I tore off a piece, a shiver ran down my spine at the soft, yeasty scent. Bread was my weakness, my comfort, and here it was, sitting between us, soft and warm, a simple pleasure we now shared.

It was a small connection, but meaningful in its own way. I watched as he reached for a piece, his movements relaxed, confident, as if he, too, found comfort in the familiar ritual. There was something endearing in the way he smiled, admitting with no hesitation that he loved bread just as much as I did. It was one of those small, human moments that made everything feel easy and natural, a quiet bond that formed over the simple act of breaking bread together.

Gato, always so considerate, began filling my plate, his hands gentle but deliberate as he placed each item in front of me. I couldn't take my eyes off him, mesmerised by his tenderness. Food had always held a special place in my heart, and the fact that he was so careful, so thoughtful in making sure I had it first and I loved it, it made me feel even more drawn to him.

At one point, he looked at me with that soft smile of his and said, "You look like someone who enjoys cooking." I smiled back, but for some reason, I told him no. It was a strange response, considering cooking had always been a kind of therapy for me. We laughed about it, it was like somehow, he knew I was hiding my cook skills, and he confessed he was a food lover. There was something so sweet, so endearing about the way he said it, and I knew, deep down, that one day I would cook for him. But in that moment, the only skills I could think of weren't in the kitchen.

As we finished the meal, we skipped dessert without a second thought. Neither of us could tear our eyes away from each other, and the tension that had simmered throughout the night was now bubbling, threatening to spill over. His gaze was locked onto mine, those captivating eyes that intrigued me from the very start. They were a mesmerising brown-greenish, but just around his pupils, a ring of honey glowed, deep and intense, like a sunburst in his gaze, his cat eyes could speak to mine; they were the window of our souls. The contrast of colours drew me in, and I could feel the air between us charged with something electric between my eyes to his.

Something electric passed between us, an unspoken exchange in the space between our eyes. It was as if I could see the very synapses firing, transmitting silent messages of desire. His presence was palpable, and it felt like his axons were reaching out, connecting to mine through that unbreakable stare. Every glance was a spark, every heartbeat a pulse in this invisible circuit between us, linking us in a way that words couldn't express.

Chapter 15
The Kisses from Heaven

His arm, already draped across my shoulder, tightened slightly, pulling me closer. The warmth of his touch sent a shiver through me, and I leant in, just enough to let him know I was ready. There was no need for words now. Every look, every subtle movement was a conversation on its own, and I hoped this Englishman would understand the silent invitation I was offering. And then, as if he could hear the unspoken desire in the air between us, he did. Without hesitation, he leant in, his hot lips meeting mine, soft yet deliberate, like everything else about him. Finally, the moment we both had been waiting for arrived, and it was perfect.

And then it was like an explosion. The heat rushing through my body, an electric pulse that started in my brain and shot down my spine, igniting every nerve in its path. My heart raced so fast I could feel it in my fingertips as they touched him. The kiss was everything—deep, passionate, the kind that felt like we'd been holding back all night, waiting for this exact moment. The world around us blurred and disappeared.

All I could feel, all I could sense, was him. His hands gripped me with a force that sent a thrill through my entire body. They were strong, urgent, like he couldn't get enough of me, like I was something he needed. His fingers dug into my arms, gripping and squeezing as if I were a lemon he was pressing for every last drop of juice—strong, intense, and deliberate. And I loved it. Every part of me responded to his touch, the intensity of it, craving more. His hands, his kiss, everything about him made me feel alive, as I was waiting for this kind of passion all my life. And now that it was here, I wasn't going to hold back, I wanted to give my all, my everything, to that moment.

We wrapped ourselves in each other's arms, and in that moment, I couldn't tell where my body ended and his began. The electricity flowed through us, our connection so powerful it was almost overwhelming. I could feel it, deep in my core, in places I couldn't even describe. It was as if I could see inside him, as though his very soul was laid bare before me. I felt like I was seeing his heart, his veins, every part of him glowing with life in blue and red colours.

When we finally pulled away, both of us breathless, he held my neck gently in his hands, his eyes still locked on mine. "Your kiss…" he whispered, his voice trailing off, unable to find the words. I could hardly speak either, my mind still spinning from what had just happened. It felt like I had returned from another dimension, a place of pure ecstasy where nothing else mattered.

And as I looked at him, I knew that in that moment, everything had changed. This was no ordinary connection, and I hoped he knew it. It was something far greater, far deeper, and as we sat there, still wrapped in each other's embrace, I realised I didn't just feel alive—I felt transcendent.

After a long, lingering kiss and a dinner that had felt more like foreplay than a meal, he leant in, smiling, and suggested we explore the venue a little. The way his eyes danced with excitement made me feel like a teenager again, high on the thrill of a first crush. We stood up quickly, laughter bubbling between us as if we couldn't contain the joy of being with one another. But as we navigated the narrow path between tables and chairs, something unexpected happened. The space was too tight to walk side by side, so I went first, threading my way between the clusters of people.

Suddenly, I felt his hand on the back of my neck—not a light touch, but firm, steady, guiding me as we moved through the restaurant. A shiver shot down my spine, catching me off guard. My thoughts immediately shifted to something more primal, something undeniably dominant in the way he held me. *Why was he doing that?* The sensation was both unsettling and thrilling, stirring something deep within me that I hadn't expected.

There was a power in his touch, not aggressive but purposeful, as though he knew exactly how he wanted to lead me. The unexpected boldness sent a wave of curiosity through me, a mixture of excitement and vulnerability. My breath hitched slightly, my mind racing as I wondered what this shift meant. Part of me wanted to question it, but the other part—the one that thrived on spontaneity, on passion—was more than willing to follow where this might lead.

My mind flashed to the idea that maybe he wasn't so vanilla after all. For a moment, I wondered if he was into something far more intense than I had anticipated. The thought lingered, and I wasn't sure how to feel about it. Man dominance wasn't usually my thing—just the idea of anything remotely painful made me cringe. But there was something about his touch, the way he held me, that stirred something deep within me, a curiosity that felt both foreign and exciting. My body responded before my mind could catch up, a warm flush spreading through me, and though there was a brief flicker of discomfort, it passed as quickly as it had come.

I decided to push those thoughts aside, refusing to let them ruin the moment. After all, tonight was about me—my desires, my pleasure. And right now, this man was everything I wanted. Handsome, charming, gentlemanly, and now with a streak of something darker, something I hadn't expected but couldn't deny I was drawn to. There was an undeniable sexiness about him, the way he carried himself with such quiet confidence. Whatever was happening between us, I knew I had to let go of my usual reservations and simply live in the moment. I could feel the tension, the pull, and I wasn't ready to let it slip away. Not tonight.

When we finally reached the dance floor, the lights were low, casting the room in an ethereal glow. The music thumped through the speakers, vibrating the air around us, but I could barely focus on it. All I could see was him—his face, his smile, his eyes shining with excitement. He looked like a young boy, filled with a pure, uncontainable joy as he pulled me onto the dance floor. His enthusiasm was infectious, making me laugh and feel completely at ease. But there was something more behind that boyish grin—a hunger that mirrored my own.

The atmosphere of the place was electric, nostalgic, like a memory of something wild and free. We danced, bodies close, but it wasn't enough. Without a word, he grabbed my hand and led me to a table in a quitter corner, away from the others. And there, in the shadows, we crashed into each other, our lips meeting in another wave of desperate, wet kisses. Our mouth were thirsty. I traced his muscles over his shirt, feeling the firmness of his chest. He was fit, toned in all the right places, and I wanted to touch, bite, and lick every inch of him.

We kissed like we were starving, and with every kiss, I could feel myself falling deeper. His hands squeezed my waist, sending sparks of pleasure shooting through me. I was overwhelmed with the need to feel him, to know what it would be like to have him pressed against me, skin to skin. My hands hovering just above where I wanted to touch most. I didn't want to go too far yet.

My body responded to his in ways I hadn't expected—urgent, craving more of him with every touch. The animal side of me, the part I usually kept locked away, began to rise to the surface, unleashed by his heat. The part of me that didn't care about being too eager, too vulnerable, too easy. All I wanted was to feel him, to taste him, to undress him and let everything else melt away. I wanted to lose myself in this moment, to let go of all the rules, and give in to the fire burning between us.

His hands roamed over my body, squeezing in ways that made me gasp. Every touch sent a ripple of heat through me, straight to the ache between my legs—a fire in my pussy made me try to open my legs as I could not even hold myself, sitting still. I could feel how wet I already was for a moment, I wondered if I had not squirted, my body responding to his every move in a way that I had never experienced before. The fire inside me was building, spilling over into him, and I could tell by the way his hands burnt against my skin that he felt it too. His body was a furnace, and I was desperate to lose myself in the flames.

Then I pulled back, my voice low and sweet. "Shall we get out of here?" His eyes were red, filled with an intensity that made my heart race. The way he looked at me, with such hunger, such need, sent a thrill through my entire body. "Yes," He breathed, barely able to get the word out. His gaze held mine for a moment, so deep it felt like he was seeing straight into my soul. There was something almost otherworldly about it, as though he was promising me a night I would never forget. And I knew, in that moment, that I didn't care what anyone thought. I didn't care if I was being too forward or too wild, noticing a group of girls seating in front of us.

We made our way down the stairs. By the time we reached the bottom, I was dizzy with desire, my mind fogged with need. Gato called for a taxi, his fingers moving quickly over his phone. The ride to his place couldn't come soon enough. Outside, the cool night air hit my skin, a stark contrast to the heat pulsing through me.

In the car, I couldn't wait. I reached up, pulling him close, my lips brushing against his neck. I trailed kisses down to his collarbone, then up again to his ear, my tongue teasing the soft skin of his earlobe. The sound he made, a deep, throaty moan, nearly pushed me over the edge. It was the sound of pure pleasure.

His moan was intoxicating, turning me into something wild, something primal. I could feel the pulse of desire between my legs, my pussy aching for release. The sweet, innocent Gatinha who had left her flat earlier that evening was gone. In her place was someone insatiable, someone who wanted nothing more than to feel him inside me, to lose myself completely in him.

He paused for a moment, looking out the window, his expression suddenly confused. Then he asked, “Should I drop you off at your place?”

I couldn’t believe the question, and without missing a beat, I replied, “We’re grown-ups, aren’t we?”

He smiled, nodding in agreement, the tension between us still simmering. And then, without hesitation, he pulled me closer again, his hand firmly gripping the back of my neck with such passion and ruthlessness that my legs instantly turned to jelly.

For a second, my eyes widened in surprise, and a sudden doubt crept into my mind. A voice in my head spoke loudly: *What if he’s a psycho? Oh God! Have You sent me a Dark Angel?*

I almost stopped the kiss right there, my heart racing, but then another voice quickly followed, teasing, “Well, Gatinha, at least you’ll die in a flattering outfit.”

So naturally, I kept kissing him. I decided to take the risk. The fire between us was too strong to extinguish now.

Chapter 16
His Cage

We finally arrived at his place, and the moment we stepped through the door, everything else faded. Each step we took felt like an invitation to close the space between us. Before he even managed to open the door fully, he pinned me against the wall, his lips crashing into mine with intensity. Every kiss devoured me; his touch was rough and uncontrollable. It was as if each kiss unleashed a wave of heat that surged through my body, setting off a chain reaction that left me breathless and my legs weak.

These weren't just kisses—they were intense, unfiltered passion, igniting desires I had long tried to keep in check. But now, with him pressed against me, all that self-control melted away. Every nerve in my body came alive under his touch, and I could feel my carefully guarded restraint slipping, replaced by a need so powerful I couldn't resist. In that moment with him, I let go of everything except the fire between us, burning hotter as we both wanted to undress.

As we got in the living room, quickly, I let my dress fall from my body, revealing my breasts. I longed for him to suck my nipples with such hunger as he kissed my mouth, his face transforming into a hungry cat as he looked at me.

He looked at me with such intensity it felt as if he wanted to penetrate me with his eyes. In one swift motion, he tore off his jumper, grabbing my waist with a force that sent a shiver down my spine. His lips moved to my neck, each kiss sending waves of heat through me as he pushed me backward, guiding me toward the bedroom with an irresistible urgency.

I could barely close my eyes, too captivated by the sight of him, my breath shallow, wanting nothing more than to keep watching him. To my surprise, there he was, his eyes wide open too, locked on mine as if sharing the same unspoken thought. But his eyes, once warm and kind, were now wild and burning with desire—a deep red that left no trace of the man I had first known.

I could feel it—the animal energy between us—and in his gaze, I saw the reflection of my own hunger, the animal inside me awakening. Our eyes mirrored one another, wordlessly telling the same truth: we were both about to lose control.

As he seated me on his bed, he pulled away to remove his trousers. My eyes could no longer meet his gaze; all I desired was to behold his naked form. I remained still, captivated by the sight before me. His body appeared as if crafted by the hands of the gods. Not only his face drove me to madness, but his broad shoulders and strong chest. I yearned to touch and feel each inch with my tongue, hands, and even with my pussy.

His perfect abs, each defined pack visible, drew my attention. Then he revealed what I had been craving—the sight of his cock. It stood before me, the object of my desire, and I was no longer the sole one hungering and thirsting for him. My pussy throbbed with hope, eager to consume him, to envelop him entirely.

His body reminded me of the wall art I used to sketch depicting Greek gods during my teenage years. My passion for Greek and Roman sculpture had materialised into reality. It felt as though a Greek god was standing before me, right there, about to take me above the clouds of Mount Olympus.

Seeing this handcrafted sculpture up close filled my eyes with pleasure, and all I could feel was my pussy rubbing against the sheet on his bed. As I pressed my pussy down, I felt so incredibly horny that I was sure he could see it all. I was there, right in front of his eyes, melting from the intense desire pulsating through me.

He wasted no time and threw his body against mine, pulling me close from my waist to the centre of the bed. My legs instinctively wrapped around his body, desperate to feel his cock against my lips. But this time, the lips I longed for were not the ones on my face, but the ones between my legs, drenched like the rain in a storm.

We couldn't even bring ourselves to close our eyes. I wanted to gaze at his stunning face, those captivating, horny eyes. I couldn't tell if he could see me through the darkness or if all he could envision was the image of my face that would forever be in his head.

As his cock yearned to penetrate me and my pussy eagerly awaited to welcome that monumental intrusion, my inner voice suddenly brought me back to reality at the most inconvenient yet crucial moment. Before the night could spiral into potential consequences, I mustered the courage to ask if he had a condom.

His response deflated my desires. “No,” he replied, bursting my balloon of lust and desire. I took the deepest breath of my life and implored him to abstain from entering me, recognising that we had only just met, despite the overwhelming hurricane of emotions and attraction.

His sweet eyes returned, offering reassurance that I didn’t need to do anything that made me uncomfortable. We shared a tender kiss, and this time, I closed my eyes as my heart transitioned from a rapid pace to a steady rhythm, my mind finding relief as if I was returning home after a long journey.

As our bodies moved in sync, like notes of a melody woven together in perfect harmony, my eyes drifted shut. In that moment of intense closeness, I felt as if I slipped inside his body, my senses heightened, running through his veins with every heartbeat. I traced the outline of his neck with my fingertips, sliding them down his back, lingering at his waist before boldly grabbing his ass. The heat between us was undeniable, like a magnet pulling us closer.

When I finally opened my eyes, there he was, his gaze soft yet intense—the kind of look that made my heart race and melted every last bit of restraint I had. His lips parted, and in a deep, husky voice, he spoke, breaking the silence between us.

“I’ve been to all these clubs, restaurants, bars…” he said, his eyes searching mine as though he was still trying to make sense. “Then I found you, right there at a bus stop. It’s like I’ve found my female version. The way you touch me, the way you kiss me… it’s exactly how I would.”

I was speechless. His words, raw and intimate, stole my breath away. It felt as though, in that moment, my deepest wish was being spoken into existence, spilling from his lips like a revelation.

Little did he know that before my day in church, I had been searching for him in the same places. All the eyes that met mine were empty, leaving me disinterested. But on that day in church, I secretly longed to find myself again. And I found myself in him. He was just like me, we connected not just in desire, but in the way we loved, touched, and kissed. It wasn’t only about attraction but about the intensity that came with it—the way we let our emotions flow freely, guiding our every move and infusing every caress with passion.

I felt overwhelmed, a wave of emotions crashing through me, because this connection wasn’t just physical. It was what our souls had been waiting for, searching for, and now we had found one another. And he was awakening parts of me I had hidden.

It felt like time had stopped. Since the moment we met that evening until now, it was as if the whole planet had frozen, locking us in our own world. But as we lay there, slowly returning to reality, I realised it was getting late, and the spell was starting to break. My flat was just across the road, so I decided it was time to leave.

We both got out of bed, the cool air a sharp contrast to the warmth we had shared, and made our way through the dim hallway toward the living room. The soft shuffle of our footsteps echoed against the walls, and as we stepped into the living room, I noticed the chaos. Clothes were scattered everywhere. I stifled a laugh, amused by the mess we'd made.

My eyes scanned the floor, searching for my dress. I found it in a crumpled heap and quickly slipped it on, but then I realised—I had no idea where my knickers had gone.

The room was dark, and I didn't dare ask him to turn on the lights. God knows what he might see if he did. I groaned inwardly, suddenly remembering my makeup. *Shit!* I thought, *my makeup must be a melted disaster by now.* The idea of facing myself in the light made me giggle nervously.

He had disappeared briefly, though I wasn't sure where he'd gone. When he returned, I was still half-dressed, fumbling in the dark, but then I spotted my knickers draped over the arm of the sofa. I couldn't help but chuckle as I grabbed them. For a split second, I wondered if I'd even worn any at all—if they had just magically disappeared. I quickly put them on, feeling slightly more composed.

As I stood, pulling my dress into place, my eyes caught sight of something that momentarily distracted me. There, bathed in the faint glow from the window, was a stunning Greek-Roman sculpture—a half bust of a man, perched gracefully on a square table by the window. The marble face, frozen in stoic beauty, seemed to watch over the room. Around it, indoor plants thrived, green and lush, just the way I loved. I smiled to myself, feeling an odd sense of comfort in this unexpected detail of his life.

I shook my head, snapping myself out of the trance, and turned toward him. He stood there, watching me with a sleepy smile. I bent down to grab my shoes and bag, preparing to slip out quietly and leave him to his beauty sleep.

He walked me to the front door, the soft click of the latch echoing in the quiet night air. I stepped onto the doorstep, turning to wave at him with a playful smile.

"Bye," I called softly, almost under my breath.

Then I ran down the steps, the cool air hitting my face as I prayed I wouldn't trip over my own feet. I wasn't quite myself yet, still floating somewhere between reality and that perfect, suspended moment we had shared.

Chapter 17
Day After the Cage

The moment I wake up, I feel the overwhelming sense of gratitude flooding my heart. As I search for my phone amidst the sofa cushions, flashes of the night before dance through my mind. The warmth in my body lingers, and as I make my way to the bathroom, I catch a glimpse of myself in the round mirror in the small entrance hall of my flat.

There she is… my face is radiant, my lips fuller, and my eyes—oh, my eyes! They sparkle like an orchestra playing their musical instruments with passion and joy.

Birds chirped in my head, and I paused for a moment, filled with gratitude, whispering my first, "Thank you, Gatinha," to myself. It felt like I was thanking my heart and soul for coming together to face the hardest battle—the one against my own reflection, my own mind.

In that moment, I realised I wasn't just thanking myself for getting through life's challenges. I was acknowledging the inner journey—the doubts, fears, and self-reflection that had shaped me. The battle wasn't with the outside world but with the beliefs and perceptions that had held me back.

My eyes linger on every curve of my body as I take in my hair, face, neck, chest, stomach, hips, and all my feminine parts. I can see and feel Gato's essence intertwined with mine, memories of a night that will forever be etched in my mind. His touch was powerful—every caress, every kiss, every bite filled with strength and fire, causing my nipples to harden and my body to remain wet with desire from our night in the cage.

I shake my head in an attempt to snap back to reality. As I gaze at my reflection, my eyes reveal everything—not just myself but something else within them—a burning brightness that I recognise. The animal within me waits patiently, ready to arise.

The buzz of my phone pulls me back to reality as I feel my feet hit the ground. The vibration sends signals straight to my brain. I know it's him. And it is—Gato, sending me a good morning text.

As I read the message, something feels different. My whole body shivers, my nipples harden, and a pulsing heat flashes between my legs. He says he's still in bed and there's space for me beside him. I laugh, shaking my head at the teasing invitation.

"Better not," I reply, my fingers tingling. "Otherwise, I won't be able to leave… I can feel the danger from here."

We exchange a few more playful texts, knowing full well that life outside that little cage was waiting. But in those moments, we didn't need to plan the next time. We both knew we'd find ourselves back in that cage soon enough. Our goodbyes leave me with a sense of peace and joy. We didn't have to force anything.

As the day unfolds, reality hits—it's my niece's birthday weekend, and there's a whirlwind of planning to be done for the party tomorrow. In a moment of spontaneity, I decide to extend an invitation to Gato. I already know his answer will probably be a polite "no," but something urges me to ask anyway.

Just as I expected, his reply comes: a gentle refusal, citing work and time constraints.

Surprisingly, I'm not disappointed. What matters is that I asked. I put my intentions out there, and I'm living in the moment. Despite the rejection, there's no bitterness, no regret. Instead, there's an overwhelming sense of freedom. I'm in charge of my emotions, my actions, and it feels powerful.

His refusal only ignites a fire inside me—a desire to seize every moment and live boldly, unapologetically. I'm not afraid to pursue what I want, and that alone brings me a new level of fulfilment. I've taken control of my life, my choices, and nothing—not rejection, not time, not hesitation—can hold me back from following my heart anymore.

This is my life, a vibrant, wild journey, and I'm embracing every beautiful, unpredictable moment it has to offer. Nothing and no one could sway me from following my heart and embracing the vibrant tapestry of experiences that life had in store.

Chapter 18
Party Time

Ready for the party, the happiness on my niece's face was contagious—a pure expression of excitement for life. She was only three, but the way she lit up a room was magic. Dressed in her pink Minnie Mouse outfit, her curly blonde hair framed her pretty little face, and her bright blue eyes sparkled with joy. Her giggles bubbled up as we walked hand in hand, admiring the decorations and greeting the guests. Her tiny footsteps pattered softly across the garden, and with every glance, her innocence and delight were like a ray of sunshine, warming my heart.

The garden was alive with energy—little blue chairs scattered around for the kids, while long wooden benches hosted the adults. Everywhere I looked, people were talking, laughing, and enjoying the day. The air was filled with the hum of conversations, children's laughter, and the subtle melody of birds singing from the trees above. Everything felt perfectly orchestrated, as if the universe itself had decided to sprinkle a little extra joy on this special day.

And the food—oh, the food! It was an irresistible feast laid out on a long, beautifully decorated table. There were Brazilian snacks of every variety: delicate pastries filled with chicken, cheese, meat, and vegetables, each bite bursting with flavour. The sandwiches were fresh, light, and made with the kind of love that you could taste in every bite. And the sweets—rich chocolates, strawberry-flavoured treats, and candies—were a dream for anyone with a sweet tooth. Then there was the cake, a masterpiece handcrafted by my little sister. It was as stunning as it was delicious, each slice moist and soft, a labour of love for her daughter's special day. The sight of it filled me with admiration, and I could almost taste the sweet frosting melting on my tongue before I even took a bite.

As I walked around, the sound of children laughing and running filled the air. There were so many kids, their tiny feet darting between the chairs, playing games, and chasing each other with pure, unfiltered joy. I found myself laughing inwardly, wondering where all these little ones came from. Their energy was infectious, their happiness contagious.

The music hummed in the background, blending perfectly with the buzz of chatter. Every now and then, a soft breeze danced through the trees, carrying with it the scent of flowers and freshly cut grass. The atmosphere was thick with the warmth of family and friends coming together. It was one of those days where everything felt right—the perfect weather, the perfect crowd, the perfect moment.

Then, my phone buzzed in my pocket. Gato. His name flashed on the screen, and though he was not physically there, it felt like he was. His message was simple, yet thoughtful—a quiet reminder that he was thinking of me. His words carried the weight of care, of interest, of respect. In his own way, he was present, and that meant more to me than he probably knew. It was like he'd woven himself into the fabric of my day, subtly, but meaningfully.

I smiled, warmth spreading through me as I responded, the sounds of the party continuing around me. I was struck by how light I felt, how content. I was surrounded by love—my family, my friends, and even Gato, who, from a distance, had shown me that he valued me in a way that felt almost divine. The universe had placed him in my life at exactly the right time, knowing this was what I needed.

I took a deep breath, feeling the sun on my skin, the soft grass beneath my feet, and the gentle rhythm of the day. I felt free, like nothing in the world could weigh me down. I watched my niece twirl around in her Minnie dress, her laughter echoing across the garden, and I realised something. This was happiness. This was what it felt like to be truly alive. Gatinha was alive, and she was embracing every beautiful, chaotic, joyous second of it.

Later that evening, the party wound down. The last of the guests had said their goodbyes, and the garden—once filled with laughter and activity—now sat quiet, bathed in the soft light of the setting sun. The decorations still fluttered gently in the breeze, a reminder of the day's joyful chaos, but it was time to leave it all behind. My feet ached from standing, and the weight of exhaustion finally hit me as I wrapped my arms around my mum, ready to head home.

We hailed a taxi, the cool evening air brushing against my skin as we climbed inside. The quiet hum of the city surrounded us, and I leant back into the seat, grateful for the chance to finally relax. My phone buzzed in my hand, pulling me from my haze of tiredness. It was Gato.

"How's the party? x"

A smile spread across my face as I read his message. The memory of the day's laughter, the children's giggles, and the warmth of family filled me up all over again. I typed back, my fingers feeling heavy with exhaustion.

"Perfect! Heading home now, I'm exhausted. x"

As I hit send, I could almost picture him lounging at home, probably nearby. He was, after all, my neighbour, and just as that thought passed, his next message came through.

"I will get my binoculars out… you might see me hovering in the window."

I couldn't help but laugh, the image of him peering out from behind his curtains making me shake my head in amusement. I fired back a cheeky reply, leaning into the playful tone.

"I saw you."

For a moment, there was a pause, and I imagined him grinning at his phone, thinking of his next move. Then, his reply arrived, and it sent a shiver through me, the teasing edge in his words unmistakable.

"Wanna see me properly?"

His words lingered in the air, curling around me like a soft touch. My heart skipped a beat, the anticipation settling in my chest. The playful banter we'd been exchanging all day had slowly turned into something else, something with an undeniable spark. I felt a ripple of excitement wash over me, the kind that left goosebumps on my skin. The idea of seeing him, knowing what that would lead to, made me smile and laugh softly to myself.

But tonight, I was too tired—my body aching from the pre-party preparations, the long day spent on my feet, and the sheer joy of the celebration. I was not at my best—physically drained, my energy spent—and I knew if I saw him now, I wouldn't have been able to enjoy it the way I wanted to. So, I gently turned down the invitation, making sure he understood that it was not about him; it was about the state I was in.

“I would have loved to,” I replied, “but I’m really tired. If you’d asked earlier, I probably wouldn’t have been able to say no.”

His response flashed across the screen.

“Ohhhhhh shit, I should have asked sooner! I’ve been thinking about it all day!!!”

I grinned, imagining him kicking himself for not asking earlier, and I replied with a soft laugh in my text.

“Exactly! Don’t think too much. Share it.”

Our conversation ended with a few more playful exchanges, the kind that left me with a lingering warmth. He wished me good night, and I returned the sentiment, the weight of the day finally settling into my bones.

As the taxi pulled up to my place, the cool night air hit my face when I stepped out, refreshing and calm. My bed was calling me, and I knew the second I hit the pillow, I’d be out like a light. My body cried for rest, and the thought of sinking into the soft, cool sheets filled me with relief. I climbed into bed, the texture of the blankets soft against my skin, and let out a long, satisfied sigh.

My phone rested on the bedside table, Gato’s messages still on my mind—a teasing reminder of what could have been. But as my eyelids grew heavy, I knew there would be more nights, more moments to share. For now, though, I let my exhaustion take over, my body finally giving in to the sweet, deep rest it craved. The day, the party, the laughter—all of it faded away as I drifted off into the kind of sleep that only came after a day well lived.

Chapter 19
Movie Night at His

At 6 a.m., the day unfolded like a deep breath, and I rose to meet it. The air bit with cool clarity, a sensation that pulled me into the present. My skin tingled as I stepped into the waking world, where butterflies swirled, their wings catching fragments of light. The morning smelled of wet earth and dew-laden leaves—fresh and grounding—as if nature itself were whispering that today held promise.

At 10 a.m., on my walk back from the gym, my earbuds pulsed with the steady cadence of a voice from a YouTube channel, sending waves of thought through me. It was more than just sound—it felt like a frequency tuned to my soul, reaching deep into my core. Everything else—the birds, the distant hum of traffic, even the comforting aroma of freshly brewed coffee from the café—faded into the background. I was wrapped in these words, their power holding me in a place of deep reflection.

I was not just here to move my body, to feel the burn of muscles in motion. This journey was not about physical strength alone. I'd been nurturing something far deeper—my mind, my spirit. The way I thought, the way I reacted—it was all changing. Where once my emotions ran wild and unchecked, they now felt like something I could hold, something I could direct rather than fear. I'd started learning to care for my mental health with the same dedication I gave my physical body. I'd shifted my thoughts, not to silence them, but to refine them, shaping them into something that served me rather than controlled me.

And more than just mind and body, my spirit had become part of this equation. There was a deeper connection now, something almost intangible but undeniable—an alignment with something greater than myself. Spiritual growth, like an undercurrent, had woven itself into my routine. It was not just about control, but about harmony—about finding peace with who I was, where I was, and the direction I was moving in.

Then, my inner voice spoke the truth that settled everything:

"The happiness of your life depends upon the quality of your thoughts." — Marcus Aurelius, *Meditations.*

The words hit like a tuning fork, vibrating through every part of me—mind, body, and soul. I'd come to realise that the quality of my thoughts shaped not just my day but my entire existence. And so, with each step, I walked in alignment—not just with my goals, but with a new sense of balance, of care for every part of me, physically, mentally, and spiritually. It was no longer just a morning routine—it was a practice, a way of being.

As I drifted into my own thoughts, lost in a quiet moment of self-reflection, the soft buzz of a message cut through the stillness. Funny enough, I knew instantly it was Gato. I smiled, already anticipating his words.

"I was thinking, so you told me to share…"

My fingers moved quickly across the screen. "Hmmmm, what's on your mind?"

He explained his week was going to be full—challenges, responsibilities, deadlines pressing down. But then, with a twist of warmth, he asked if I wanted to meet that evening. Maybe watch a movie. The moment he suggested it, I knew we wouldn't really be watching anything. We both knew that. He was happy to try, though, which only made it sweeter. Our messages turned playful, flirtatious, the chemistry sparking as easily through words as it did in person.

But I had to tell him the truth. "I got my period this morning, so… I won't be able to do all the things I wanted to do with you tonight."

I held my breath for his response. It came quickly, and it didn't disappoint. His interest was clear—direct, but caring. He wasn't fazed. He wanted me, *all* of me. My body, yes, but also something deeper. It was like our souls were calling out to each other, some invisible thread pulling us together.

"We can kiss," he replied.

The simplicity of it made my heart skip. His words made me feel wanted in a way I hadn't expected, and I found myself smiling, reassured by his tenderness. I said yes, of course. We didn't need to dance around our feelings or play games. It was all honest between us—raw and real. What he didn't know, though, was that he was more than just a connection. He was a gift from the universe, a gift from God. And soon, he'd realise it too.

The days passed and the evening finally arrived. I chose something simple and comfortable—a long, ivory wool dress. The summer heat in London had eased, leaving the night air crisp with an unexpected chill. I liked the way the fabric felt against my skin—soft and light, almost like a second layer of protection. I didn't need to call an Uber or walk far, just across the street, but I wrapped the dress around me a little tighter for comfort.

Gato messaged, "Do you want anything?"

I replied with a grin, "Just you," knowing it would make him laugh.

He replied, "Welcome to Brazil." His reply was sweet, playful. It reminded him of that night at our first dinner when I had teased him with the phrase—a kind of welcoming him to my World.

When I arrived at his door, I texted him. I couldn't even remember his flat number. But then, through the glass front door, I saw him. There he was, striding towards me, jeans hanging just right, a simple white T-shirt clinging to his chest. God, I had missed him—his face, his eyes, his body. The sight of him stirred something deep within me, making my stomach flip with nerves and desire. He opened the door, and before I could say anything, he pulled me into his arms. His kiss was intense, urgent, like he had been waiting just as long for this moment. His hands found my waist, drawing me closer as he led me inside.

As we settled in, he devoured a burger while the TV flickered with muted images in the background. The smell of the burger filled the air. I watched him, absorbed in the ordinary moment, and suddenly he mentioned he was moving out.

Surprised, I blinked at him, trying to mask the confusion creeping in. *Why hadn't he told me before?* The thought nagged at me, a whisper of insecurity I didn't want to entertain. I quickly pushed it aside, refocusing on him. He explained his situation, and it made sense. It was a big flat for just one person, after all.

He finished his meal, and we shared glasses of water. Gato took his plate to the kitchen, and I turned my eyes to the TV, where an image of a crackling fireplace danced on the screen. Moments later, he returned with a small speaker, and soon, the soft hum of rock 'n' roll filled the room. The music played, but I couldn't focus on the lyrics. My attention was all on him—his movements, the way he spoke, the timbre of his voice, that delicious British accent curling around his words like music of its own.

The room felt warmer, the soft glow from the TV casting shadows that danced along the walls. Every brush of his hand, every glance felt electric. The smell of his skin and warm and familiar, making me want to lean in closer.

I could feel the pull between us, stronger now. We didn't need to speak; our bodies did that for us. This wasn't just about desire—it was about something deeper, a connection that neither of us could deny. And as the night stretched on, with the soft hum of music and the heat of his presence, I knew he felt it too.

We kissed with a fervour that bordered on desperation, each touch sending electric currents through our bodies. Every touch was a spark, every movement igniting something deeper. The heat between us simmered and boiled, building to an explosive peak that left us breathless. As I slid my dress off, my skin tingled, the warm air enhancing the fiery desire that raged within me. Exposing my breasts to him felt like unveiling a precious treasure, his eyes devouring every inch of my exposed skin.

I wore nothing but a pair of tiny cotton box knickers—delicate but suggestive. His eyes darkened with desire, and I could feel his body tense undermine as I straddled him, taking control.

I wanted him exposed. I needed to feel his bare skin beneath my fingers, to see every inch of him vulnerable to my touch. My hands moved to his T-shirt, pulling it off, revealing his toned chest. He didn't resist—didn't even hesitate—just let me undress him completely until he was naked for me.

As I hovered above him, I felt a rush of power, my legs straddling his hips, watching the way his face softened as he surrendered to my control. I could feel how hard he was beneath me, the heat of him pressing against the thin fabric of my knickers as I gently rubbed my wetness against him.

He moaned softly, a sound that drove me crazy. My mouth watered with the desire to taste him, to take him in. I leant forward, my lips brushing against his, teasing, before trailing down to his neck, his pulse racing beneath my tongue. I could smell him—clean—making me dizzy with lust. I kissed my way down to his chest, biting gently at his nipples, drawing a gasp from his lips.

The feel of his chest hair, though trimmed, drove me wild. The animal inside me was waking up. I imagined how much more I would love the feel of it if it were thick, natural, a sign of his raw masculinity. My nails traced over his skin, loving the contrast between the smoothness of his muscles and the slight roughness of the hair. But I wanted more. Needed more.

My kisses trailed lower until I was on my knees in front of him, looking up into his eyes. His breathing had changed, deepening, becoming ragged, and his chest rose and fell quickly as he anticipated what was coming. His eyes burnt, a flush creeping up his neck as his pupils dilated. The tension between us tightened, vibrating like a cord pulled too taut.

I could hear his heartbeat thudding, loud even against the backdrop of the soft rock music still playing. His breath was uneven, his lips parted as he exhaled deeply. The sounds that escaped him—low, guttural groans—made me tremble with excitement. They were primal, wordless, the kind of sounds that come from deep inside when there's nothing left to hold back.

I leant in closer, my lips grazing the heat of his skin, and the sound that tore from his throat made my spine arch. He knew what I was about to do. I could see it in his eyes—dark with need, his desire almost tangible, vibrating in the air between us.

His eyes grew heavy, his breath catching in his throat. I could feel the energy pulsing between us, every nerve in my body on fire, every sense heightened to the point of breaking. His skin was warm under my hands, and I could smell the musk of his cock mingling with the scent of my own. Time seemed to stretch out, the moment hanging in the air, electric, as I let the anticipation build between us like a tidal wave, ready to crash down and consume us both.

I started to lick around the base of his cock, teasing him, blowing a mix of cold and hot air from my mouth, letting him feel the temperature change against his heated skin. His cock twitched as my tongue found his balls, gently circling them, while my hand wrapped around him, slowly stroking. The smooth, rhythmic motion of my hand built the tension between us, and I kept my eyes locked on his, knowing how much he loved it—how much I loved it. The connection between us was magnetic, every movement deliberate, every stroke a silent message of control.

He couldn't taste me tonight, couldn't eat my pussy the way I knew he wanted to, but I had him. He was mine, completely at my mercy, and I relished the power. I let my tongue travel back up to the tip of his cock, savouring the sweetness of him before I took him fully into my mouth. His cock filled me, hard and thick, and the taste—so intoxicating—was like a rush of sweetness. I sucked him deep, swirling my tongue around him like I was indulging in the most decadent vanilla ice cream.

His body responded immediately. His hips jerked, lifting off the sofa as if trying to push deeper into my throat, desperate for more. His skin flushed, turning a shade of red, his face contorted in pleasure as he let go, lost in the sensation. The deeper I went, the more intense it became—my mouth growing wetter, sloppier, as I took him deeper into my throat.

I could feel the weight of his hands on my head, pressing me down against his cock, my lips stretched tight around him. Each time I pulled back, I could feel the slick trail of my saliva coating him, making him slide more easily back into my mouth.

I placed both hands on either side of his hips, bracing myself as I fucked him with my mouth. His moans grew louder, like an animal. He grabbed my hair, pulling it back so he could see my face, watching me with dark, lust-filled eyes as I took him all in, my mouth swallowing him down until he was fully inside me. His cock filled my throat, and I could see the way his expression shifted—his lips curling, eyes narrowing as though he wanted to devour me in return. His face twisted with raw hunger, like an animal on the verge of losing control.

His moans turned into guttural sounds, his breath quickening, and he tugged me up suddenly, crashing his lips into mine. His kiss was rough, needy, tasting himself on my lips, a mix of lust and control passing between us. But I wasn't done with him yet. I pulled back, my eyes fixed on him, and went back down to where I belonged, my mouth wrapped around his cock once more. This was my focus, my pleasure, his lips forgotten as I worked him with everything I had.

I could tell he was close—his body tensed, his breathing laboured, his hips thrusting involuntarily as if trying to hold back the release he couldn't contain. The sound of my wet mouth, the slick movements of my lips and tongue, filled the room, louder now than the music still playing in the background.

His cock slid easily in and out of my mouth, my saliva making everything smoother, wetter. It felt incredible—his hardness against my lips, the way he stretched my throat. I could feel him everywhere, the taste of him lingering, intoxicating me further.

I wanted to taste his release, to feel him spill inside me, to swallow every drop. But not yet—not tonight.

I knew this wasn't the moment. I wanted that final act when we were both completely lost in each other. But for now, I pushed him to the edge, my hand and mouth working together, moving faster, deeper. His cock throbbed, and I could hear his breath catching in his throat, his body jerking as he fought to hold back.

The wet sounds of my mouth and his cock filled the room, the rhythmic suction echoing around us, mixing with his moans and the soft rock still playing in the background. My mouth was soaked, my tongue sliding easily around him as I took him deep, his cock pressing into the back of my throat.

Every time he thrust, I could feel my own body responding—my pussy slick and wet, aching for him, as if the pleasure I gave him mirrored back into me. It was like rain between my legs, my pussy dripping, as I brought him closer and closer to the edge. And I knew, when the time was right, I'd take everything he had to give, but not yet…

Chapter 20
Second Dinner Date

My mornings were far from what they used to be a couple of month ago. There was more in the air—*Was it love? Could it be?* I decided, yes. After all, I was in control of my life, of my feelings, of my thoughts. It is my life, and I chose to see it with the eyes of a child, where everything sparkled with wonder. All I wanted to see were colours, melodies in the air, and lyrics that seemed to dance on the wind.

It is love because it came wrapped in the form of a human. *My gift, delivered by angels, and how could I not love it? How could I not feel my heart stir with excitement when something so unexpected, so pure, came into my world?*

I met someone who, in a way, realigned my heart and mind, helping me untangle emotions I didn't even know were knotted up. It was a dramatic transformation that began to change everything—not just in my mind but throughout my entire being. Gato, with his joy, brought love into my life in a way I had never experienced before. He made me feel it in a new way, allowing me to fully embrace it. In doing so, he helped me uncover something deep within myself that I knew it was missing.

His love was the spark that reignited what had long been dormant. And because of him, I didn't just feel love—I learnt how to give it back, not only to him but also to myself. His presence reminded me that I was worthy of kindness, both from others and, most importantly, from myself. And by learning to love myself, I became a better person for him.

I had been waiting for someone to notice me, to hear me, to remind me of my own worth. And he did just that, with his child spirit, so much like my own. He reminded me to look into my own eyes, to see that everything I wanted—my dreams, my desires, my future—started from there.

And as I sat there by the window, having my black coffee, lost in thought, 07.43 a.m., the soft buzz of a message on my phone snapped me out of my thoughts, pulling me back into the present. My heart quickened, an instinctive flutter I had come to recognise. It was him. I reached for my phone, already feeling the warmth of anticipation bloom in my chest.

Gato's message:

"Morning, neighbour. Hope you have a wonderful day xx. Can't wait to see you x."

I smiled, my heart doing a little dance as I read his words. My reply was quick, almost instinctual, mirroring the excitement I felt inside.

"I can't wait to see you either."

Time had a strange way of slowing down when you were waiting for something—or someone—special. Days felt like years, and yet the hope made everything feel brighter, more alive. We had made plans to meet for dinner earlier that week, and this time, Gato was keeping it a surprise. He wouldn't tell me where we were going, only the time he'd pick me up.

The mystery thrilled me. I could feel excitement bubbling up, making it hard to focus on anything else. The day stretched on, every hour dragging its feet as I tried to keep myself occupied, but my thoughts kept drifting back to him. The feel of his presence lingered in my mind, like the echo of a song you couldn't stop humming.

There was a crispness to the air, the subtle promise of evening as the sky began to dim, teasing the edge of dusk. I could feel the flutter of butterflies in my stomach back again. My body hummed with excitement, my mind racing through all the possibilities. *Where could he be taking me? What surprises did he have in store?*

I reminded myself to hold my horses, to savour the slow build-up to the night ahead. There was a certain magic in the waiting, in letting the anticipation stretch just a little longer. Tonight would be special—another evening where every moment felt new, like a blank page waiting to be written on.

The night was young, and so were we. *Why not?* Age is just a number, after all. It had no real weight, no real meaning, when your heart feels light and your spirit free. With Gato by my side, it felt like the world had opened up before us, every corner filled with secrets and adventures just waiting to be discovered.

Together, we were stepping into something unknown, yet it felt familiar—like home. We had all the time in the world, and tonight, that world was ours.

At 9.08 p.m., he was already waiting for me, I felt beautiful, so beautiful that night. I wore a bronze, long dress, tight on my body, exposing my curves. I could not even breathe or walk in that dress, but it was amazing. I felt amazing. I did my hair up, tied this time, the fringe on the side held behind my ears. I wanted him to see my whole face—the face that he could not stop calling "pretty face." Every word, every compliment he made, filled my heart with love. He was so kind. He was gorgeous himself. I believe, for this reason, he had no problem on expressing his feelings and letting me know that he found me beautiful.

As I stepped outside the flat, there he was, waiting by the taxi, his familiar figure standing tall in the evening glow. Just like before, Gato moved with ease, opening the door for me, his eyes warm, making sure I was comfortable. But this time felt different. There was an intimacy, a closeness between us know that hadn't been there on our first dinner.

I wrapped my arms around him, pulling him tight, feeling the soft press of my body against him, my dress clinging a little too snugly. I felt my breasts nearly spilling from the fabric, and yet, all I could think about was how close we were.

He, ever the gentleman, didn't want to ruin my makeup. Instead of kissing me on the lips, he leant in and pressed his lips to my neck—oh God, not the neck. I giggled, the sensation sending shivers through me, making me laugh in spite of myself. He chuckled softly too, his hand guiding me gently to the seat, making sure I was settled.

As we both sat in the back of the taxi, I could feel his eyes on me, staring with such intensity that I felt my cheeks flush. I wasn't used to feeling shy, but with him, I could be. He had this way of making me self-conscious in the sweetest way, as if I was seeing myself through his admiring eyes. His words were nothing but compliments, a steady stream of praise that both flattered and embarrassed me. His gaze, his upper-level sophistication—it was like something out of a movie. And there he was, dressed in a crisp white shirt, looking every bit the leading man. So chic, so handsome. My heart skipped a beat.

He leant in closer, a mischievous smile playing on his lips, and finally told me where we were going—Roka on Charlotte Street.

"Have you been?" he asked, his eyes watching my reaction closely.

I smiled, answering truthfully. "Yes," I said, and I could see his face fall just a little. He had wanted to surprise me, to be the first to take me there.

I quickly explained, telling him that it had only been with family. I added, "This is my first time here, with you. The first time that matters."

His expression softened. I wanted to make sure everything about this night was perfect, to show him that this moment—this experience—was ours. It was special because it was with him. And as we rode through the dimly lit streets, I knew that whatever happened next, it was already perfect because we were together.

Roka on Charlotte Street was even more beautiful and romantic than I had imagined. The moment I stepped inside, I realised this was actually my first time at this particular location. The atmosphere was intimate, yet alive with energy. As we walked toward our table, the hostess complimented my dress with a warm smile. I loved it—and Gato heard it, too. We exchanged a knowing glance, both aware of how good we looked together. I could feel the eyes of others in the restaurant following us, admiring us. And you know what? Yes, we were the most gorgeous couple in the place. It's my story, and I'll say it—on that night, we were the most gorgeous couple on the planet.

Walking to our table felt like stepping onto a catwalk. Every step felt deliberate, every glance filled with admiration. But Gato wasn't content with the standard arrangement of sitting across from one another. Oh no, he wanted to be right next to me. Without hesitation, he asked the hostess if we could sit side by side, and she found us the perfect spot—a cosy corner where we could watch the chefs expertly prepare our food. It was perfect.

As I settled into my seat, I felt Gato gently pull my chair closer to his, closing the space between us. And then, without hesitation, he kissed me. I melted right there in that moment, everything around us fading into a soft blur. I didn't care about the food, or the conversation, or even the beautiful restaurant. I could have easily run back to his place then and there, but I played it cool. It was absolutely perfect.

As the evening unfolded, we talked. We shared bits of our lives, and stories of his world. I was curious to hear more about him—what he hoped for, what he wanted. But I stayed away from talking about my past. I had made a conscious decision to leave it behind, to live in the present. It had become my new philosophy. The past was irrelevant to me, just a collection of lessons learnt.

There was nothing there I could change. It was out of my control. I accepted it, and I was done with that. I wasn't interested in rehashing old stories. The past no longer defined me. What truly mattered was who I was in that moment: free, open, and ready to embrace the life that was unfolding before me. And sitting next to Gato that night, I felt more certain than ever that everything was falling into place, exactly as it should. The only thing that mattered was the present—the moment I was sharing with Gato.

At some point during the evening, I told Gato about the wish I had made to God, that I wished for him. I wasn't sure if he was really listening, lost in the easy rhythm of our conversation, but I said it anyway. I wasn't about to keep anything inside. I wanted him to know how much I liked him. I had made that clear from our very first dinner.

I was happier than I had ever been, and he was a big part of the reason for that. Gato had helped me find my way back to life. He didn't even know the impact he had on me; didn't realise how much he had changed the rhythm of my days. And now, here he was, sitting next to me, the man who had unknowingly breathed new energy into my world.

I had promised myself, and God, that I would be open to receiving love. That day in church, I had made a vow—I was ready. Ready to embrace whatever life had to offer. Now, sitting beside him, I felt that this moment was a part of that promise being fulfilled.

I remember telling him, *I don't know about you, but I crossed an ocean for you.* And it was true. England wasn't my home—Brazil was. But Brazil had always felt too small for me, too limited for the life I envisioned. Even as a child, I knew I was meant for something beyond its borders. Somewhere along the way, I had gotten lost, but Gato had helped me find myself again.

So, in that restaurant, surrounded by the soft murmur of conversations blending into the background, all I wanted was him. To be fully in that moment with him, enjoying every second. I just wanted to enjoy the night, to talk, to kiss, to hug and feel free. And that was enough.

From that moment on, I made a silent promise to myself. Every time I with Gato, I would forget about everything and everyone. I would live each moment with him as if it were our last day together, as if time itself could pause and we would exist only in the now. No past to haunt us, no future to worry about—just us, here and now, wrapped in the fleeting beauty of each encounter. Life is too short to hold back, too precious to be spent anywhere but in the present. And every moment we shared were a gift, one that I was determined to fully embrace. The rest was up to the universe.

Chapter 21
His Cage Again

As we stepped outside, he led me to a secluded spot where I could sit and wait while he called for a taxi. Under the enchanting glow of the moonlight, we shared a tender kiss. London was graced with a beautiful summer night. The air was warm and inviting, setting the perfect scene for a night of romance.

Our embrace was filled with passion as we kissed, held each other close, and playfully teased one another. We lingered in each other's arms until the taxi arrived, aware that the night ahead held promise of intense heat and desire.

I couldn't help but feel a pang of sympathy for the cab driver that night. Our chemistry was undeniable, and if the driver hadn't been present, we might have succumbed to our impulses right then and there in the backseat of the car. I was no longer shy in my desire for him, feeling the hardness of his cock pressing against my hand. The image of him naked sent shivers of anticipation through my body. Each kiss ignited a spark within me, his lips and tongue sending waves of pleasure through me.

As I tried to distance myself slightly to regain composure, I caught a glimpse of the driver's stoic expression in the rearview mirror. I couldn't help but feel a twinge of guilt for the poor man, caught in the midst of our undeniable attraction.

Getting out of the taxi and into his flat felt like the longest journey, even though it was only a few steps. The anticipation between us was almost unbearable, every glance filled with unspoken desire. I could feel my own wetness, the heat pooling between my thighs, as we finally stepped through the door.

The world closed behind us. We were on each other—our lips and tongues locked together, desperate and hungry. There was no hesitation, no time wasted. Our hands moved quickly, undressing each other as if every second apart was too long. The air was thick with the need to feel, to taste, to touch. My body ached for him, and I knew he felt the same. Our soul needed one another.

His touch was electric, and as his hands roamed over my bare skin, I couldn't help but crave more. My body was trembling, my pussy wet and aching. I needed him inside me—needed to feel his cock, to be stretched by him, to lose myself completely in his arms.

As we fell onto the couch, our bodies pressed together, I could feel the hardness of his cock against me, and the anticipation of what was coming made my breath catch. His eyes met mine, and we didn't need words—our minds and bodies were in perfect sync. I lost myself in the sensation, my vision blurring with desire.

He knew exactly what I wanted, and I knew he wanted the same. The foreplay had been a mere prelude to what I truly desired—his cock. I yearned for that powerful presence to fill me, to stretch me to my limits. I wanted him to feel the heat emanating from my core, the fervour of my desire burning uncontrollably.

When I felt the head of his cock at the entrance of my pussy, a shiver of pleasure ran through me. The wetness, the heat—it was everything he craved. Slowly, he pushed inside, and my body responded instantly. The sensation was overwhelming, my hips arching as he filled me, stretching me in the most delicious way.

The room was filled with the symphony of our bodies—his deep moans harmonising with my newfound vocalisations. I had been quiet for so long, but now all I wanted was to let go, to release the pent-up desire that had been building within me. The sound of my voice, exclaiming "Aye, Aye," mixed with breathless gasps, echoed off the walls.

Every movement, every sound that emerged from our entwined bodies—the symphony of our voices, the heat between his cock and my pussy—all ignited waves of pleasure within me. The intensity surged with each powerful thrust, my heart racing in sync with his, the connection between us deepening with each shared breath. In that moment, it felt as though we were merging into one, our souls intertwining in the fiery passion of the night.

The way his body moved against mine, the way he filled me completely, made everything else disappear. All that existed was him, the pleasure, the feeling of being so close, so connected. I wanted more, needed more, and as he pushed deeper, I knew that this moment was ours—a perfect merging of desire and emotion. My hands slide through his back; I could not resist touching each inch of his body.

As each forceful thrust propelled us deeper into a tempest of ecstasy, our bodies melded in a symphony of desire. In that fleeting moment, he possessed me, body and soul. The raw intensity of our connection left me breathless, our hearts drumming a primal beat in unison.

Our lips collided in a searing kiss, a desperate attempt to fuse our very essence in a whirlwind of longing. The primal need coursing through me was undeniable as my pussy clenched around his hard cock, yearning for more, aching for his touch.

Ensnared by sensations that transcended reality, I found myself lost in a whirlwind of movement and sound. It was as if some unknown force had taken hold of me, drowning me in the fiery depths of our union. The climax that swept over me was a tidal wave of pleasure, unrelenting and boundless.

As the orgasm surged through me, my hands tried to find his as he held me by my hands against the sofa. My body responded in ways I had never known; a yell came out from my mouth. I felt like an animal—all I wanted was to squeal. I felt my soul coming out from my body. I could not see or hear anything anymore. I was so horny. Waves of ecstasy rippled through every fibre of my being, sending tingles of pleasure cascading down my spine. My skin hummed with the electric charge of desire, every inch of me vibrating with sensation. The pulsing of my pussy intensified. My clit, my nipples were so hard as I felt his hard cock deeper inside me—a seductive dance of pleasure that echoed through the room.

Struggling to open my eyes, I gazed through blurred vision at Gato's face. Those cat-eyes were not his anymore; his animal was patiently waiting to emerge. His eyes bore into mine, a mix of pleasure and a hint of possessiveness that gave me shivers. I had to recompose myself while he grabbed me by my waist and pulled me up to stand, ready to take me to his cage—his bedroom. I could barely walk, but he led me through the corridor, my feet not even touching the floor. He threw me onto his bed, then, after a hot kiss on my lips, he moved down to the lips between my legs.

He ate my pussy with his mouth in such intensity that I felt my body begin to tremble, signalling I was about to come again. I had to lift my head to watch him, his mouth full. The sight was so arousing that I couldn't contain myself, succumbing to another intense orgasm. My juices flowed into his mouth, my own mouth watering in response. I moaned with pleasure as he expertly ate my pussy with his mouth.

As his body slid against mine, I was still trying to come back to life. I felt the weight of his body as he put my legs up on his shoulders and penetrated me so deeply. He had a hungry look on his face. He began to breathe harder, his cock pulsing inside my pussy, signalling his was about to come. His body moving in rhythm as he drove his cock deeper into my soaking pussy.

He couldn't hold back any longer. With a guttural yell of pleasure, his eyes turned, and finally, he came intensely, spilling his seed all over my stomach and breasts. I reached for his face, pulling him close to me, and he let his body weight rest on me as we stayed there, embracing each other until we could compose ourselves.

Chapter 22
Awakening in His Arms

Listening to his heart still racing as I rested my head on his shoulder, his arms wrapped around me gently and sweetly, I felt like I had found home. I lost myself in the comfort of those arms, but then the thoughts in my head started shouting at me, pulling me out of that peaceful moment. *What do I do now? Should I get dressed and go back to my flat? Should I stay?* The confusion swirled, loud and insistent. It was as though he could hear the debate in my mind because he suddenly asked, "Would you like some water?"

"Yes, please," I answered quickly, eager for a distraction as I stood up. I felt like a child, overwhelmed with too many toys, not knowing where to start. While he went to fetch the water, I hurried to the bathroom, needing a moment to check my state. In front of the mirror, I laughed at myself—my cheeks flushed a deep red, my skin glowing. I noticed that all my cheeks were blushing, even the ones hidden under the sweat and heat of the night. A mix of our perfumes lingered on my skin, and I inhaled deeply, wanting to keep that scent with me forever.

Still, I knew a shower was necessary. I wasn't sure if I was staying the night or not, and that uncertainty weighed on me. The thought of sleeping together made my stomach churn with unease. It was not about him; it was about me. I wasn't someone who easily fell into sleep next to another person; I woke up frequently, restless. And then the voice in my head piped up again—*What if he snores? Oh God, no!* I couldn't help but laugh at myself, at how ridiculous my worries were, while my hair clung to my face, wild from the hours of kissing and everything else.

When I emerged, he handed me the water, his eyes warm and sweet. I asked if I could shower, and without hesitation, he went to grab clean towels for me. "This way," he said, leading me to the bathroom just behind his bed. I hadn't even noticed it was there earlier. A quiet surprise swept over me—I was being upgraded. His bathroom, not the one in the hall I'd been using before. It was a subtle but significant gesture, one that made me laugh quietly to myself. *He's letting me in*, I thought. There was something intimate, almost sacred, about this small transition. It wasn't just a bathroom; it was a piece of his privacy he was offering me. I didn't take that lightly.

As he handed me the towels, I couldn't help but admire his thoughtfulness. He was kind and gentle, moving with that same effortless grace that had drawn me to him in the first place. And even though my mind was still spinning with overthinking, I didn't want to leave. Part of me worried about intruding on his space, but a stronger part of me knew—I wanted to stay.

After the shower, I found him lying on the bed, waiting for me. The sheets smelled fresh, and the room was filled with a soft, comforting silence. I slipped into bed beside him, his arms opening to hold me once more, and I felt at peace again. That moment—his touch, the warmth of his skin, the steady rhythm of his breath—was all we had, and I wanted it to last as long as it could. The uncertainty was still there, lingering in the back of my mind, but in his arms, it didn't matter. All that mattered was now.

He had fallen asleep, so quiet, so peaceful, while I lay wide awake. I shifted gently, moving away from him to give him space. As I watched his face, my heart swelled. *Oh God, he's so handsome*. His nose, his beard—oh, that beard that I couldn't stop running my fingers through all night. His lips, slightly parted, inviting—everything about his face was perfection, crafted by the hands of God Himself.

Then, in his sleep, he turned around, nuzzling into it. I smiled, amused and charmed by the simple movement. *This is my cute,* I thought. It was time for me to try and sleep too. But as soon as I settled in, the nightmare of restlessness began. I lay there, trying not to disturb the serenity beside me, staring up at the ceiling. His bed was enormous, enough room for both of us to move around without ever touching, so I positioned myself all the way to the left. Still, sleep wouldn't come. My mind raced in the dark, flashes of the night replaying in my head, my thoughts refusing to settle.

And then, the inevitable. The call of nature. I tried to ignore it, tried to will it away, but it was no use. Desperation started creeping in as I silently prayed to God for help. Please, not now, I begged in my mind. But the pressure was too much to bear. I had to get up.

Carefully, I slipped out of the bed, trying not to make a sound. The room was unfamiliar in the dim light, and anxiety pulsed through me. His en-suite bathroom was just behind the bed, and though I could've taken the longer journey down the hall to the other one, I couldn't risk waking him by wandering through his flat.

So, I groped around in the darkness, fingers skimming the walls, searching for the light switch. My pulse quickened, frustration growing as I failed to find it. *Where is it?* I cursed under my breath. The door. Oh, that damn door. It was so heavy, refusing to close properly. Panic rose as I tried to push it, but the door remained stubborn, creaking ominously.

In a mixture of thrill and anxiety, I decided to use the bathroom in the dark, with the door wide open—because, of course, the door wouldn't budge. I tiptoed inside, feeling my way along the walls, trying to make as little noise as possible. But the second I sat down, the sound of my pee hitting the water echoed like a cannon through the silence of the flat. It was so loud, absurdly loud in the stillness of the night. *Oh God, is this really happening?*

I bit my lip, trying desperately not to laugh at how ridiculous it all was. *He's definitely going to wake up.* My heart raced as if I'd been caught in some grand act of mischief, and with every second that passed, I was sure he could hear everything. This has to be the longest pee of my life.

Finally, I finished, but just as I thought I was in the clear, the next wave of panic hit me—*I have to flush*. My eyes darted around the bathroom, looking for an escape, but there was no avoiding it. I couldn't just leave it! I cursed under my breath, inching towards the flush handle like I was defusing a bomb.

The second I pressed it, the toilet roared to life, as if mocking my attempts to be discreet. *Oh no, no, no!* The sound reverberated through the flat, louder than anything I could've imagined. I squeezed my eyes shut, cringing at the noise, heart pounding, and praying with every fibre of my being that he was still fast asleep.

I hurried back to bed, my pulse racing like I'd just escaped some absurd midnight heist. I pulled the covers over me, but my mind continued its relentless churn. I counted stars that didn't exist, replaying the moments of the night, every touch, every kiss, over and over in my mind. Sleep felt so distant. I reached out for my phone to check the time, but then I remembered—I had no idea where my bag was. No way to reach my phone, no way to distract myself from my spiralling thoughts.

I turned to face him again. His chest rose and fell with each peaceful breath, and I watched, unable to tear my eyes away. He looked so good, so serene. For a long while, I just stared at him, taking in the way his lips barely moved as he breathed. He was perfect.

Eventually, slowly, I felt my own eyelids grow heavy, and the sleep that had eluded me for so long finally arrived, pulling me under as I watched him sleep.

I jolted awake to a sudden fart noise, unsure whether it came from me or from him. I chuckled quietly, thinking it was probably me. Just as I was starting to drift off again, another noise—definitely not mine—broke the silence. This time, it was unmistakably him. My silent laughter shook my entire body as I tried not to make a sound.

Sleep was now a distant dream. I lay there, staring at the ceiling, my mind racing as I tried to find a comfortable position. As I shifted around, I noticed his face was just inches from mine.

I couldn't help but wish to kiss him and get close to him, but I didn't want to disturb his sleep. So, I remained still, my eyes fixed on the morning light gradually brightening the room. The sun was rising, signalling the start of a new day, but for me, it was just a morning of trying to get comfortable in the aftermath of an unexpectedly noisy wake-up call.

As I stared at his face, his eyes slowly began to open. His hand instinctively reached for mine, and without hesitation, I found his arms, curling myself into him like a child seeking the comfort of a protective embrace after a nightmare. I squeezed between his arms, letting myself melt into his warmth. In that moment, I felt a freedom I was looking for my whole life—a release from the confines of my own mind.

I was in love—completely and utterly in love. But it wasn't a love filled with chaos or urgency. It was pure and calm, like a soft breeze on a still night. I didn't need words; I didn't need to explain or define anything. Our eyes spoke for us, carrying all the understanding and tenderness that words would've only diminished. He didn't need to say anything, and neither did I.

In the quiet of that moment, I knew he was the one. I had no doubt. But he still needed to find that answer for himself. There was no rush, no pressure. I wasn't worried or anxious about the future. We didn't need to force anything, didn't need to follow any timeline. I trusted in something bigger than us, something divine. All that mattered was this moment, wrapped in each other's arms, where everything felt right, as if we had found the missing pieces of ourselves in each other.

And, well, we all know what happened next. His hand moved over me, familiar and tender, and in the soft, quiet haze of morning, he pulled me back to him. Before I could even process it, the heat between us flared up again—his body hard against mine, his cock pressing into me, rekindling the fire we had stoked the night before.

My pussy was still sore, every nerve sensitive from the intensity of our previous night, but I didn't want to stop. I craved more. His deep, steady breaths mixed with mine, his pace driving me to the edge once again. With every thrust, the aching pleasure built until, finally, I came around his cock, my body quivering in release before I could slip away, leaving the sweet, intoxicating warmth of his arms.

I had to escape from that animal before he completely destroyed me. We both stumbled our way to the bathroom, laughing in breathless exhaustion. Oh my God, my face—pale as the white walls of his flat, drained of all colours. *Where was the blood in my face*? I caught sight of myself in the mirror and couldn't help but laugh at the mess of it all. My hair was wild, sticking up in every direction, but I didn't care. The only thought running through my head was, *Where's the blood?* My lashes were so heavy I could barely open my eyes.

And then there he was, coming up behind me—naked, gorgeous, looking impossibly sexy. His body stood tall behind mine, the contrast between my pale face and wild black hair only made the moment funnier. We locked eyes in the mirror, and despite how dishevelled I looked, we both smiled. There was something beautiful in the chaos of it.

We both liked what we saw—two bodies, two souls intertwined in ways that went beyond just the physical. We belonged to one another, and we knew it. Our bodies fit together perfectly, like two pieces of a puzzle, creating a kind of living art. We were a masterpiece, a wild, untamed wall of perfection, and somehow, despite the exhaustion and madness, it all felt just right.

Chapter 23
Mysterious Event

It was a peaceful Sunday morning, the kind that eases you into the day, and I found myself thinking of Gato. We often connected through messages and unspoken thoughts, a quiet but constant rhythm between us. I was preparing for a quick workout at the gym before my day started—family responsibilities already waiting for me. There was a chance I might see him that day. We had exchanged a few texts earlier, something that had become second nature by now.

We didn't meet every day, of course; life outside our little world—"our cage"—kept us both occupied. But on this particular Sunday, he was supposed to have the day off, and we'd promised each other that our next meeting would be somewhere public, to ensure we kept our hands to ourselves. The thought made me laugh because we both knew how impossible that would be, but we were happy to try anyway.

As the day unfolded, I received a message from Gato:

"Today is running away from me a bit, Gatinha; 'How was your gym?'"

He explained that his day off was slipping away, overtaken by obligations, and meeting up wouldn't be possible.

Gato: "Yeah, I have roar issues for the week, so looks like I have to go to… tomorrow… just sorting through… client at 2.00… Did I tell you about… ?"

Gatinha: "Okay. No worries at all, you got do what you have to. x"

The message didn't bother me. I had family plans, too, and it was perfect timing to shift focus back to them. Gato was grateful for my understanding of his hectic schedule. What he didn't realise was that he embodied one of the very things I had once prayed for: "Someone driven and focused on success, even if it meant having little free time."

At that moment, I wasn't working, but work had always been my priority, my anchor. I wanted someone who understood that drive, who valued time spent being productive and focused on building a future. And there he was—so consumed by his own goals that he barely had time to catch his breath. And somehow, that made him exactly what I had hoped for.

The morning passed as smoothly as the warm sun that stretched across the quiet streets. After finishing my workout, I felt light, my steps almost floating as I made my way back to my flat. The day was sunny, one of those rare London days where the sky is clear, and Heath St was alive with the gentle hum of life. The breeze was cool, but not biting, and I savoured the stroll up towards Holly Hill, my mind pleasantly wandering.

Halfway there, just before turning onto Holly Hill, I saw him. It was Gato. Or at least, I thought it was him. He was a little way ahead, turning the corner, his figure unmistakable even from a distance. He wore skinny sweatpants, cinched at the ankles by bright white socks, a slim white T-shirt hugging his frame, and a red and white cap, worn backwards like a little boy. Someone was walking behind him, but all I could focus on was him.

For a split second, I wanted to call out his name. My voice nearly broke the quiet around me, but something stopped me. As I watched him, a thin stream of smoke curled into the air, rising slowly in the bright sunlight. My steps faltered. "Don't shout," my inner voice warned, so I didn't. I slowed my pace as I realised—*was it a cigarette? Or maybe a vape?*

My thoughts raced. I couldn't remember if he'd ever mentioned smoking. There was never a trace of it on him, not on his lips, not on his breath. I racked my memory, trying to recall any moment where I might have caught a hint of it, but nothing came to mind. And yet, there he was, disappearing around the corner, and in that fleeting moment, I felt the weight of uncertainty settle over me.

Had I ever asked God for a partner who didn't smoke? I remembered praying for someone who avoided alcohol and drugs, someone grounded. But had I ever thought to ask for someone who didn't smoke? The question buzzed in my mind, but then I smiled. Of all the things I'd prayed for—qualities like integrity, ambition, kindness—I hadn't asked for someone good-looking. And yet, there he was: a striking, sexy, English man, far more than I could have hoped for in so many ways.

I thought of all the good in him, the qualities I had already begun to notice and cherish. *Would smoking really be enough to upset me?* I wasn't perfect myself, after all. I'd promised to embrace this gift with an open heart, to love and care for it as it came. His imperfections didn't shake what I felt for him. If anything, they made him human, just as flawed and complex as I was. I trusted God, trusted the universe, trusted the feeling that had been building between us. It was too precious to let something like this create doubt.

Maybe my inner voice had stopped me from shouting his name to spare him any embarrassment. Perhaps he had his reasons for keeping it from me, or maybe it wasn't even mine to worry about. The moment passed, and I decided not to dwell on it. There was still so much we didn't know about each other, so much new ground to cover. One day, I knew he would tell me, or I'd see it for myself. But that day wasn't today.

I didn't want to let something as small as smoke cloud the beauty of what we were building. I let the thoughts slip away as I continued my walk home, choosing instead to focus on all the reasons I had to be grateful for him, for us. It was too soon, too tender to let anything taint it. Smiling to myself, I headed towards my flat, the warmth of the sun on my skin a reminder of the good things still to come.

By the end of the day, as had become my habit, I found myself scrolling back through Gato's messages, reading and re-reading them, enjoying every word. His words had a way of wrapping around me, drawing me closer to him even when we were apart. I was sitting with my mum, distracted by her conversation with my brother on speakerphone, when my finger slipped, and suddenly, I realised I had accidentally called him.

My heart skipped a beat. *Oh, God!* I panicked and quickly cancelled the call, sending him a message right away to explain that it had been a mistake. To my relief, he was his usual kind self, replying almost immediately, saying he would call me back soon. And true to his word, he did.

It was the second time I'd heard his voice over the phone. Our relationship had lived in the world of messages, typed words and silent exchanges while apart. But when his voice finally came through the line, sexy, low and smooth, it hit me like an electric shock in my pussy that made me smile, laugh even, with the sheer pleasure of it. His voice was so sexy, so unexpectedly intimate, and I wanted to tell him what it had done to me. But with my mum over the phone with my brother nearby, their conversation buzzing around me, I held back. Our moment was private, too intimate to be shared amidst family chatter.

We spoke briefly, his voice a caress even through the phone, and before we hung up, he asked if we could meet in a couple of days during the week. It would be a little late, he explained, as he was busy between work and moving flats and wouldn't be free until later in the evening. But he made it clear that he wanted to see me, and asked if I wanted the same. Of course, I did. The thought of seeing him again stirred something inside me that hadn't quite settled since the last time we'd been together.

Friday night was still fresh in my mind, my body still holding the memory of him, and the days without him had stretched too long. I missed him—more than I expected to, and more than I wanted to admit. Smiling to myself, I agreed, knowing that Tuesday couldn't come soon enough.

Chapter 24
Whispers of Love and Morning Magic

At 3.30 a.m., I woke with a start. My eyes snapped open, fully awake, as though some invisible force had shaken me from sleep. The room was cloaked in darkness, thick and still. I glanced around, disoriented, half-expecting the clock to read midnight or maybe 1 a.m. at the latest. But no—it was 3.30 a.m., that strange hour hanging between night and morning, neither here nor there. I lay still, trying to settle back into sleep, but something was pulling at me, nudging me. Staying in bed felt impossible, like an invisible hand was pushing me out from beneath the covers.

Confused, I swung my legs over the side of the bed, my feet landing soundlessly on the cold floor. The world outside my window was pitch black, but I could hear foxes rustling and yipping in the distance, their eerie calls slicing through the stillness of the night. I moved through the dark, ghostlike, to the bathroom, splashing cold water on my face, hoping to shake the strange restlessness from my bones. The icy water shocked my senses awake. I brushed my teeth absentmindedly, not daring to make coffee—it was far too early for that, even for me. All I needed was water, something pure to ground me.

I wandered back into my room, feeling the gentle tug of the early morning hours, and as I passed the door, my gym clothes caught my eye, hanging there patiently, waiting. For some reason, my inner voice whispered, "Go for a walk." It wasn't a suggestion. It felt like a command. Without thinking, I peeled off my pyjamas and slipped into my gym outfit. The air outside would still be cool, I imagined, so I grabbed my oversized university jumper, its worn fabric soft against my skin. As I laced up my trainers, I could feel the anticipation building, like my body knew something special was about to happen. I filled my water bottle, popped in my EarPods, and checked the time. 4.45 a.m. The perfect moment to catch the sunrise.

Summer mornings have an electric quality—the air is chilly but not enough to bite, just enough to fully wake you, to remind you that life stirs just below the surface. I left the flat and stepped into the stillness, the streets deserted except for the occasional hum of a distant car. Primrose Hill was close by, and I knew it would be the perfect place to watch the sky change from black to gold.

The streetlights flickered softly above, casting a dim glow over the empty roads. It felt like the world was mine, a private moment untouched by time or anyone else's reality. With Savage Garden playing softly in my ears, I felt an overwhelming sense of lightness, as if I could float above the pavement, free from everything. I probably looked ridiculous, half-dancing, half-walking along the street, but I didn't care. There was no one around to see me except the shadows.

As I approached Primrose Hill, my heart quickened. I climbed slowly, enjoying the crisp morning air as it filled my lungs, the smell of dew and grass sweet and fresh. The sun was just beginning to edge above the horizon, casting long, golden fingers across the landscape.

I stood there at the top of the hill, the world spread out before me, bathed in soft, pale light. The city below was still sleeping, but up here, it felt like I was witnessing the birth of something new, something pure and untouched. I closed my eyes for a moment, the warmth of the rising sun kissing my skin, and I let out a breath I hadn't realised I was holding.

The song lyrics still played softly in my ears, but now they felt like something more—like my own private conversation with the universe. Each word seemed to echo back at me, filling the air with a deeper meaning. I stood there, watching the first light of dawn touch the horizon, and felt an overwhelming sense of gratitude. I was awake, fully awake, not just in body but in spirit. It was as if the clarity I had been searching for was suddenly unfolding in front of me, like a door opening to something far bigger than I'd imagined.

In that moment, I knew—I was being called to something greater, something more profound. I could feel it, this energy humming inside me, a certainty that something special was about to enter my life. My mind, once clouded with doubts and uncertainty, was now clear, sharp. I could see my future, not in specific details, but as a vision of purpose, an awakening that stirred deep within. It was powerful, like the rush of wind before a storm, a force that I knew came from love. And I didn't question it. There was no fear, no second-guessing. I simply stood there, staring at the sky, and whispered a quiet thank you to God.

Then, louder, with conviction, I spoke into the stillness, "I'm ready. For everything that's meant for me, for whatever my purpose is. I will follow every sign, face every challenge." My voice echoed faintly in the open air, mingling with the sound of the world waking up. I felt lighter, freer. It reminded me of that day in church when I'd let go of my worries, when the fears and confusion that had been suffocating me were suddenly lifted. I had unblocked myself that day—my doubts, my beliefs about love had shattered. In their place was a love so pure, so encompassing, that it filled me completely.

And Gato—he had helped me see that. He had shown me, in his quiet, unassuming way, how effortless love could be. How easy it was to show care, to express emotions without fear. He made me feel safe, comfortable, like I could be my truest self without the need to hide or shield my heart. From the very beginning, I hadn't held back. I made it clear that I liked him—no, that I loved him. And somehow, I didn't need to say it in words. I knew he could feel it.

Love was in the way I spoke to him, the way I listened, the way I cared. It was in every small detail, every shared moment, every glance. And I realised that love was less about words and more about actions, attitudes, the energy between two people. I was learning that—learning that love could be silent but still loud, unspoken but still heard. And in that quiet morning, standing alone at the top of the hill, I felt loved. Not just by Gato, but by life itself. By everything, everyone around me, and especially by "ME," since "I love myself."

I was blessed to feel it, even in its silence, even in the solitude of the early morning when no one else was watching. And as the sun broke fully over the horizon, bathing the world in golden light, I smiled. I was ready—ready for whatever was coming next. Ready to live with love in every moment.

As I stood atop the hill, bathed in the morning light, memories of my time with Gato drifted back to me. His laughter, warm and quiet, echoing in the back of my mind; the way he'd look at me, his gaze soft but intense, as if he was seeing parts of me, I hadn't yet seen myself. It was like he was right there, in this golden dawn, filling the air around me with something I couldn't quite name.

A soft breeze stirred, carrying with it an unexpected sense of him, and I found myself whispering his name into the morning. I didn't know if he'd ever hear it or even feel it, but in that moment, it felt enough that I could.

I took in the world around me, the awakening sky, the quiet of the city below, and felt my pulse quicken, realising that in some way, every step forward felt a little like stepping closer to him. And maybe that was the feeling that had pulled me out of bed this morning—a pull stronger than restlessness, as if something or someone was calling me toward something just beginning to unfold.

Chapter 25
The Moment We Became Gato and Gatinha

Late in the evening, we had planned to meet at his flat. The connection between us was growing stronger, pulling us together like a magnetic force. We craved each other's presence. The days, the hours leading up to our meetings were filled with a sweet kind of anticipation. We were always so excited, so eager, and we could never wait to be near each other again.

As I arrived at his place, the door was left open. A small detail, but it felt like an invitation, a silent beckoning into his world. I stepped inside, feeling the air thicken with his presence even though I couldn't see him.

"Hello?" I called softly, the sound of my voice breaking the silence.

Then he appeared, his face lighting up with that gorgeous smile I loved so much. That smile that made my heart race every time. Before I could say anything more, he closed the distance between us, and we kissed. It wasn't just a kiss—it was hungry, urgent, like we were starving for each other. His lips pressed against mine, and I felt the familiar pull. Every time we were together, it was as if gravity itself shifted. It was impossible not to want to tear each other's clothes off the moment we touched.

I had promised myself, once again, that tonight would be different. I would say hello, keep things calm, and we would talk—really talk, like two people getting to know each other. But as soon as our bodies were close, words became unnecessary. His touch spoke louder than any conversation ever could. We couldn't help ourselves. I wanted to talk, to ask him about his life, to hear the stories that made him who he was. But as his hands moved over me, every thought seemed to melt away, replaced by a burning need.

We tried; we really did. We played with restraint, teasing the idea of just sitting down and having a conversation like normal people. But the truth was, it was hard to keep our clothes on around each other. The air between us was thick with desire, and once again, we found ourselves tangled in each other, skin on skin, breathless and unable to stop.

I couldn't complain. I loved being touched by him, loved how he made me feel like I was the only person in the world. But there was a part of me that wanted more. I wanted to hear his voice say something other than "Baby" in the heat of the moment. I wanted to know him, the real him, beyond the fire that flared every time we met.

But tonight wasn't the night for that. Tonight was just for us, for the way we made each other feel alive, even if we barely spoke a word. The words would come later. For now, it was enough just to be with him, to lose ourselves in each other again.

There I was, riding him on the sofa in the living room. We had started with a plan, something simple—just watching a movie together. But like every time we were alone, the air between us had other ideas. My eyes locked onto his, and I could feel him so deeply inside me, every inch of him filling me. I moved in just the right way, the way that made my clit rub against him. His eyes, usually so full of heat, had softened, growing hazy, almost innocent.

He looked defenceless beneath me, like a man who had surrendered completely to the moment. And maybe he had. I knew I was in control—of him, of this moment. I was already his owner, in a sense, though I wasn't sure if he realised it yet. Maybe he did. Yes, he did. He couldn't tear his eyes away from my face, his gaze full of awe, as though I was some vision he couldn't believe was real.

I loved the way he made me feel, the way his words slipped out so easily, always telling me I was beautiful, how my smile lingered in his mind long after I'd left. He wasn't afraid to say what I needed to hear, to express every thought, every feeling. And his openness—his vulnerability—made me feel alive in ways no one had before. In such a short time, he had done something to me that others couldn't manage in years. It was impossible not to fall for him, not to care deeply for the man who made me feel so cherished.

Then, in that moment of pure intimacy, his voice cracked the silence.

"I love you," he moaned softly, the words rolling out of him almost unbidden. My heart stopped. My face must've betrayed me, freezing as the weight of those words settled over us. He must've noticed because he quickly corrected himself, "I love this."

But I wasn't sure if I heard right, probably I did not. The word "love" had hung in the air, and even if he tried to cover it up, I knew. He didn't need to say it out loud—I already felt it in every touch, in every kiss. And without saying a word, I kissed him back, gently, my lips brushing against his, my fingers tracing the outline of his jaw. I didn't need him to repeat it. Love was there, between us, whether we said it or not.

That night was sweet, tender even, after we had taken each other to the stars and back. I called him "Gato." He smiled, his eyes lighting up with curiosity, and asked what it meant. I explained, telling him that in Brazil, we call a handsome man a "Gato," like a cat. He had jumped into my life so unexpectedly, so gracefully, like a cat sneaking into a room without anyone noticing. And he was beautiful, no question about that.

He loved the nickname, repeating it with a grin that made my heart swell. Then, he asked, "What about for a woman?"

I smiled, enjoying the way he looked at me as if he couldn't get enough. "Gatinha," I said. And that was it—our little secret names for each other. From that moment on, we called each other "Gato" and "Gatinha," and every time the words left his lips, it was like a soft caress, sending a warm rush of affection through me. It wasn't just a nickname—it was ours.

As the night wore on, I realised it was getting late. I didn't want him to be exhausted for work the next day, so I reluctantly decided it was time to leave. He asked if we could meet over the weekend, and I said yes, but we didn't need to make specific plans. We both knew it would happen. It always did.

I gathered my things, gave him one last lingering kiss, and left the flat. As I descended the stairs, I turned back, catching one last glimpse of him standing at the door, bathed in the soft glow of the hallway light. His smile was perfection. He grinned, that gorgeous smile of his spreading across his face, and I felt my heart swell once again.

"Bye, Gato," I called up to him, my voice echoing in the stairwell.

There he stood, his eyes following his Gatinha walking away, disappearing into the dark night.

Chapter 26
Embracing Harmony: Making Peace with My Inner Child

Every morning had become the best part of my day, but this one was more than especial special. It marked a month since I surrendered myself to God, and my heart was overflowing with gratitude. So much had changed since that day—my life had taken a new course, one filled with light and purpose. As I left my flat in the early morning darkness, I pulled on my favourite running outfit: a black long-sleeved top that clung to my skin and black leggings that made me feel strong and sexy. The air was cool against my face, carrying with it the smell of damp streets and the quiet hum of a city still asleep.

I started walking, the rhythm of my feet tapping softly on the pavement. My music played through my headphones, filling the silence with a pulse, a beat that synced perfectly with my steps. The music took hold of me, urging me forward in a way that felt almost magical. I don't know if it was the song, the stillness of the darkened streets, or the quietude of that early hour, but something in the air shifted. There wasn't a soul around, just me and the world still wrapped in night's embrace.

Without thinking, I began to dance while I walked. My body moved freely, guided by the rhythm, my arms swaying, my hips moving with each step. The music filled the air around me, and suddenly it wasn't just sound—it was colour, swirling in the darkness like invisible paint, vibrant and alive. The world around me was no longer black and grey; it was filled with light and energy. I felt it—this incredible sensation building inside of me, a warmth spreading through my chest until it felt like I was glowing. It wasn't just the music or the movement. It was love, pure and simple, exhaling from every part of me.

And here, alone in the quiet streets, my steps became more fluid, more deliberate. My movements were sensual, as if my body was no longer my own, but something instinctive. I was like a sleek, sexy black cat prowling through the shadows, owning every inch of the ground I covered. The darkness wrapped around me like silk, and I moved through it effortlessly, each step a dance, each sway of my hips its own kind of music.

It felt surreal and funny, like I was the only creature alive in a world that had stopped just for me. I felt free, utterly untethered. Like an animal, wild and alive, just like the foxes I saw ahead. They darted through the street, playing in the shadows, rummaging through rubbish as if they owned the night. One of them stopped, its red eyes gleaming as it stared directly at me, unafraid, curious. For a moment, it felt like we understood each other—two creatures of the dark, wild and unbound by the rules of the waking world.

I carried on, my body still swaying to the beat, dancing past the fox without a care in the world. The freedom I felt in that moment was unlike anything I had ever known. It was as if nothing could touch me, nothing could break the spell that had been cast over me. I was alive, truly alive, and I didn't care who saw. I didn't care about anything but the music, the love radiating from me, and the feeling of being utterly, completely free.

As I reached the top of Primrose Hill, the city of London stretched out before me, cloaked in the deep blue darkness of early morning. The view always took my breath away—the lights of the city glittering like stars fallen from the sky, scattered across the ground. The sight was unreal, almost magical. I stood there, mesmerised, soaking in the beauty of it all, feeling the cool air brush against my skin. In that moment, I felt like a black cat perched high on a rooftop, watching the world beneath me, quietly owning the night.

My life played like a movie in my mind, a reel of memories and dreams. I remembered climbing onto the roof of my childhood home, sneaking away when no one was watching, just to dance alone under the open sky, singing without music—just the one in my head. I would twirl and move, my body free, my spirit wild. I used to sit on the edge of the roof, legs dangling over the side, the ground impossibly far below. Fear always whispered at the back of my mind, but it was that very fear that kept me there, enjoying the rush of adrenaline, as if I were floating—my feet barely tethered to reality.

Now, standing on the top of Primrose Hill, I felt like I had unlocked something deep inside me. The past came flooding back, and with it, the little girl I had once been. She had been forgotten, left behind on that rooftop long ago, but in this moment, it was as if I had set her free. I saw her, dancing through different places and times, a part of me that had always been there, waiting to be rediscovered. The sky above was bright, alive with possibility, and in these moments, I felt like I was touching something just beyond the ordinary, the same magic that once filled my childhood.

That little girl, who used to love pink, she knew that one day she'd be on top of the world, looking down at the city, feeling that same thrill of freedom and possibilities. And now, standing there on Primrose Hill, it was as though my childhood dream had come true. I was exactly where I was meant to be, watching the city from above, just like I had always imagined.

God has a plan for everyone, I thought to myself. We just need to talk to Him, then open the eyes of our hearts to see the signs, just like the children do. Hence, we can truly understand His guidance. The path was always there, even when I couldn't see it clearly, and now, in this moment, I could feel that everything had led me to this point. My future had been written long before I realised it.

But as I grew older, I had lost touch with that part of me. Yet, somehow, Gato—with his playful, childlike spirit—had helped me rediscover that lost part of myself. His energy, his joy, had reawakened that girl who used to believe in magic, in endless possibilities.

I smiled to myself, feeling a sense of peace and clarity wash over me. The city below shimmered, alive with stories yet to unfold, each light representing a life in motion, a journey in progress. And in that moment, I knew—my story had already begun. It was my year, and everything was falling into place, with the certainty that this was just the beginning.

Chapter 27
Unexpected Visit

Monday morning arrived, the day before my mum's departure back to Brazil. I woke early as usual, the sky still draped in soft shades of dawn, somewhere between deep indigo and ash grey. I decided to prepare an especially heartfelt breakfast for her—simple, yet exactly how she loves it. I could already imagine her smile as I set to work, slicing fresh, warm bread that steamed lightly as I spread butter over it, watching the golden melt pool into its soft surface. The kitchen was quiet except for the rustle of the bread's crust under my knife and the occasional soft clink of ceramic plates.

The rich scent of coffee soon began to fill the room, dark and strong, cutting through the morning's stillness. It was the kind of coffee you could feel—the bitterness sharp on the tongue, earthy and fragrant. I brewed it slowly, knowing the aroma alone would be enough to wake her, pulling her gently from sleep. As I poured it into her favourite cup, I arranged everything on the small, round glass table by the window—the table where I often sit in the mornings, watching the sky shift from night's deep navy to the subtle greys and blues of a waking city. The light was soft, filtering through the curtains like a whispered invitation for a peaceful morning.

Every detail had to be perfect, like one of the soap operas we used to watch together as a family back home. I smoothed the tablecloth, set out the cutlery just so, and placed the buttered bread on the plates. Everything looked as it should, but it was the meaning behind it all—the love in every small gesture—that made it feel like something more.

As I sat there, reflecting on how much had changed, I thought about the happiness I had longed for over the years—the moments of joy that now seemed so present, yet so fleeting. The room smelled like fresh bread, butter, and coffee, a comforting mixture that held memories of home. My chest swelled with gratitude, for the day, for my mum's presence, for the life we shared, however brief these visits might be.

Then I heard her soft footsteps. She appeared in the doorway, her smile lighting up her face in that way only she could. Her eyes, soft and knowing, flicked from the table to me, and for a moment, we just looked at each other. Her smile was so tender, it nearly brought me to tears, but not from sadness—no, it was something deeper. Joy. Nostalgia. The ache of impending separation. But all I could feel was happiness that she was here, in this moment with me.

I knew this was emotional for her too—her last days with family in London before she'd return to Brazil, where my dad was waiting, missing her in the way only someone who's spent over forty-five years of marriage with their soulmate could. It must be so hard, I thought, to be apart after building such a beautiful life together. My dad, a tall, striking Greek man who had once crossed oceans to find her, now waiting for her return.

And here I was, repeating the same patterns, having crossed my own oceans to find my love, decades later.

Afternoon settled in, the light outside shifting from golden to soft amber as I received a text from Gato. It was a simple, caring message—he wanted to know how I was feeling, knowing that my mum would be leaving the next day. It was such a sweet gesture, and in that moment, I couldn't help but feel a surge of happiness. His presence in my life was something different—steady and comforting in a way that filled spaces I knew were empty. I was alone, even though I often convinced myself I was not. I had a wonderful family, close friends, but with him, there was something more—a sense of completeness, of peace, like a missing piece quietly sliding into place.

I had been missing him. The weekend had been devoted entirely to family—gatherings, conversations, the kind of time that made me feel both full and wistful. Gato had been busy too, with work and his own commitments, and I knew he needed his energy. But still, we both felt the absence. When I least expected it, my phone lit up again. Another message from him, asking if I could meet him quickly as he was passing by my flat on his way home from work. My heart raced with excitement. I didn't even have time to think about what I was wearing, let alone change—I was shaking with anticipation, a buzz of adrenaline coursing through me. Without a second thought, I hurried out, leaving my mum packing her luggage.

I rushed down the corridor, my footsteps echoing off the walls as I hit the stairs, not caring about the noise or the fact that I was in a tiny pair of shorts and a barely-there top, my skin tingling in the cool air. My top was almost translucent, clinging to my body and revealing more than I would have normally felt comfortable with, but I didn't care—I just wanted to see him. I reached the first-floor landing and paused by the large window overlooking the street. I scanned the sidewalk below, eager to catch sight of him before I reached the ground floor.

And there he was, walking with that boyish, almost shy gait, his eyes darting around like someone passing by their first crush's house, hoping for a glimpse of her. My breath caught in my throat, a rush of warmth flooding me. I flew down the remaining stairs, my legs trembling with each step, and found him waiting at the door, his eyes lighting up the moment he saw me.

Before either of us could speak, his mouth was on mine. The intensity of his kiss took my breath away, his tongue pressing deep into my mouth, tasting of warmth and desire. It felt as though he was pulling me into him, his need as desperate as mine. I could've kissed him for hours, that familiar heat building between us as his lips moved with mine. I grabbed the back of his neck, my fingers threading through his hair as I pressed myself against him. He pinned me against the wall, the rough texture of the brick cool against my exposed skin, but all I could focus on was the feel of his body, his cock pressing against me through his trousers.

Our breathing was ragged, every glance, every brush of skin against skin enough to ignite us both. His hands roamed my waist, and I could feel the electricity between us switched back on—dangerous, undeniable. I knew we were in the middle of the building, where anyone could walk by, but I didn't care. I just wanted him, every inch of him, to stay locked in this moment. The world could've disappeared, and I wouldn't have noticed, lost as I was in the taste, the smell, the heat of him.

His kisses were relentless, consuming, the kind that left my lips tingling and swollen long after they'd ended. We stood pressed against each other, locked in a heated embrace, our bodies alive with the kind of urgency that makes time disappear. My breath was uneven, matching the rhythm of his. Slowly, the world outside of us began to seep back in—the cool draft against my bare skin, the muted sound of doors closing somewhere in the building. I pulled away just enough to meet his gaze, my fingers still tracing the line of his jaw, feeling the warmth of his beard beneath my fingertips.

The space between us was thick with unspoken need, a magnetism that made it impossible to break the connection. I swallowed the lump in my throat, heart pounding, and then, almost tentatively, I asked, "Do you want to come over to my place for the first time?" My voice was soft, intimate, barely more than a whisper. I bit my lip, feeling the pulse of my own heartbeat in my ears as I added, "My mum leaves tomorrow, and I'll be alone. I'd love to make dinner for us—just the two of us."

For a moment, he seemed caught off guard. His head tilted back against the wall, his chest rising and falling as if to steady himself after my invitation. The playful heat in his eyes softened, replaced by something tender, something raw. His smile—oh, that smile—was boyish, almost innocent, the kind of smile that makes you feel like you're sharing a secret with someone for the first time. His lips parted as though he might say something more, but all that came out was a simple, "Yes." His voice was eager, almost breathless. "Could it be tomorrow?"

I blinked, surprised by his immediate excitement. I hadn't expected him to want this so soon. But in truth, I was thrilled by it—by the thought of seeing him again, by the closeness I craved with every part of me. "Tomorrow, then," I said, unable to stop myself from smiling back, my heart swelling at the thought of him in my home, of the meal I would prepare, of the night that could unfold between us.

But just as the moment deepened, the sharp creak of a door at the far end of the corridor snapped us back to reality. Footsteps echoed off the walls, growing louder as a neighbour approached. Panic surged through me as I remembered how little I was wearing—my tiny shorts, the sheer top that left almost nothing to the imagination. I felt the heat rise in my cheeks, a mixture of embarrassment and amusement. Without thinking, I ducked behind Gato, pressing myself against his back in an attempt to hide. My skin tingled as I leant into him, the cool fabric of his T-shirt brushing against my bare stomach.

Gato tried to appear composed and unfazed, though I could see the corner of his mouth twitch with barely-contained laughter. He stood there, casually leaning against the wall, his hand slipping into mine to give it a gentle, reassuring squeeze.

The neighbour passed by, thankfully oblivious—or perhaps politely pretending not to notice the flushed faces and the awkwardness of the moment.

The hallway suddenly felt too bright, too exposed, the air heavy with the scent of lingering cologne and the subtle, metallic tang of old building walls.

As soon as the neighbour pass through the front door, disappearing from sight, I stifled a nervous giggle. Gato's eyes met mine, and the tension, the heat that had simmered between us, surged back in an instant. We didn't need words. Our glances said everything.

I bit my lip, pushing him gently toward the door. "You should go, before something more happens," I whispered, my voice playful but shaky with the excitement still buzzing between us. He laughed, a low, teasing sound that sent another thrill through me, and I gave him one last soft push towards the exit. He lingered for a second, his eyes tracing over me as though trying to memorise the moment, then finally, he gave in and stepped outside.

We both laughed at the ridiculousness of the situation—half-dressed, flushed, caught in the heat of the moment like teenagers.

As soon as I closed the door, I sprinted up the stairs, my heart racing, cheeks flushed. I could still feel his gaze on me, and when I turned to look back down, there he was, standing in the doorway, grinning as he watched me disappear.

I opened the door to the flat, my heart still racing, and the moment I stepped inside, I caught the look on my mum's face. She was sitting at the table, checking her phone, trying to suppress a knowing smile, her lips twitching at the corners as if she was trying not to laugh. Her eyes sparkled with the kind of understanding only a mother could have.

I felt my cheeks warm under her gaze, but I couldn't help smiling too. "He was downstairs… just for a minute," I said, my voice light, trying to sound casual but failing miserably.

She didn't say anything, just gave me a look—the kind of look that said everything. I didn't have to explain anything. She knew. She had seen it in my eyes, in my flushed cheeks, in the way my breath hadn't yet settled. The way I was still caught up in the afterglow of Gato's kiss.

We shared a quiet smile, a soft moment of recognition. She knew I was falling, deeply, and completely in love. There was no use denying it.

Without a word, we turned our attention back to packing her bags. The quiet rustling of clothes and the gentle clinking of zippers filled the room, but my mind was elsewhere—still downstairs, still lost in the taste of Gato's lips, the way his hands had held me so close.

I tried to focus on the task at hand, but my thoughts kept drifting to the next day. The dinner I'd promised him. Our first real night together, just us. What would I cook? Something delicious, more than special, something that would capture this new tenderness between us. I could still feel his kisses lingering on my skin, making it hard to concentrate, my heart already planning the evening ahead.

And all the while, my mum said nothing. She didn't have to. She simply let me float in my thoughts, her silent smile knowing more than words ever could.

Chapter 28
My Cage My Rules

The day began with a hint of magic in the air, the kind of morning where everything feels possible, and you can almost hear the hum of excitement beneath the stillness. I woke up with a quiet smile tugging at my lips, knowing that today would be the day I would spend with Gato. As the soft sunlight filtered through my curtains, I stretched lazily in bed, feeling the warmth of the moment seep into my bones. I lingered for a moment, savouring the anticipation like the first sip of a rich black coffee—which was exactly what I indulged in next.

The coffee was perfect—bold and smooth, with just the right hint of bitterness. I could feel the heat of the cup radiate through my hands as I sat by the window, lost in thought. Outside, the sky was painted in soft shades of morning blue, and I felt as if I were floating among the clouds, already dreaming of the night ahead. A special night, one I was determined to make perfect. My mind drifted, plotting the evening's menu in delicious detail—every dish carefully chosen, every flavour planned. From starters to dessert, every bite would speak of love and care. And, of course, I smiled to myself—the best dessert would be me.

With a contented sigh, I got dressed, slipping into something light and comfortable for the warm day. The sun was already high, casting a golden glow over everything as I stepped out and made my way to Hampstead Village. The world seemed to sing around me—the sky a flawless blue, the heat of the sun already warm on my skin. I could feel the gentle breeze on my face, as the sound of my favourite music filled my ears. Each lyric seemed to match my mood, and before long, I was humming softly to myself, walking in rhythm with the beat.

I probably looked ridiculous to the people passing by, smiling broadly and swaying ever so slightly to the music, but I didn't care. Happiness surged through me, so pure and bright that it felt as if everyone around me could sense it. And perhaps they could. I noticed a few people glancing at me with soft smiles, as if they could read my thoughts and knew what was coming—knew that this day, this night, would be unforgettable.

As I wandered through the village, I revelled in the simple pleasure of picking out the best ingredients, touching the textures, smelling the freshness of each item. I stopped by my favourite butcher, and the scent of freshly cut meats mixed with the earthy smell of the market around me. I could practically taste the grilled prawns I planned for the starter—marinated in a vibrant mix of fresh herbs and garlic, paired with warm, crusty bread. For the main course, I imagined the baked salmon, perfectly tender, its flavours infused with the sweetness of roasted vegetables. And for dessert, something light and cool—Greek yogurt topped with a luscious berry sauce and a sprinkling of pistachios.

I wanted it to be perfect. Every dish would be a gift, a way to show him how much I cared already. I pictured the way he'd look at me across the table, the warmth in his eyes as he tasted the food I had made with such intention. I wanted him to feel at home, to sense the care and affection behind every bite. Through the meal, I wanted him to feel the warmth of family, the beginning of something real, something lasting.

The day passed in a whirl of excitement, and as the evening drew near, I returned home, eager to begin the final preparations. The food was ready, the table set just as I had imagined—dark blue plates that reflected the candlelight, soft sunflower that added a touch of elegance, and the gentle scent of lemongrass from my diffuser filling the air. The atmosphere was perfect, intimate, with low rock-and-roll music playing in the background, setting the tone for the night to come.

I took a deep breath, the anticipation bubbling inside me like champagne, and made my way to the shower. The cold water cascaded over me, soothing and refreshing at once, as I feel my hot blood so close to my skin. I had chosen my favourite shower gel—one that smelled of passionfruit and lemon, the scent bright and tantalising as it filled the air around me. I closed my eyes, imagining how the night would unfold, how his hands might explore my skin later, gentle but insistent. I laughed softly to myself, feeling a flush of warmth and joy as the water ran down my body. The thought of him made my heart race.

After turning off the water, I stepped out and towered off slowly, savouring the moment. The bathroom was filled with the fresh scent of citrus, the mirrors slightly fogged from the steam. As I stood in front of the mirror, I took my time moisturising my skin, letting my fingers glide over each curve, admiring the softness, the way my body felt under my touch. In that moment, I felt alive, sensual, every inch of my skin tingling with the thought of what the night would bring. I could almost feel his hands in place of mine.

I smiled at myself, shaking my head with a soft laugh, reminding myself to stay in the moment, to let the evening unfold in its own time. But even then, I couldn't help but feel the excitement rise again, that quiet, powerful thrill of knowing that soon, he would be here with me, sharing this perfect night, this perfect moment.

With one last glance in the mirror, I left the bathroom, the scent of passionfruit and lemon lingering in the air, mingling with the promise of what was yet to come.

The sudden buzz of the building door made my heart leap in my chest. Gato had arrived. In that split second, excitement and nerves swirled together, sending butterflies tumbling through my stomach. I could feel the anticipation build as I stood frozen for a moment, not knowing what to do. *Should I wait here, composed and calm? Or should I throw caution to the wind and run to him down the corridor, wrap my arms around him the second I saw him, and tell him how much I had missed him?*

For a moment, I imagined it—the sound of my footsteps echoing in the hallway, the rush of his arms wrapping around me, and the warmth of his embrace. But something held me back. I wanted this moment to unfold with care, savouring each second. So, I decided to wait inside, my hands lightly smoothing down my dress, trying to calm the thrill racing through my veins.

I heard his footsteps approaching the door, my heart pounding with each step closer. Then, finally, I opened it, and there he was, standing in front of me, looking more gorgeous than I could have imagined. His presence filled the doorway, his eyes warm and bright as they met mine. For a moment, neither of us spoke, just drinking in the sight of each other. He smiled and said, "Hi," in that familiar, soft voice, and it made my stomach flip. He held a couple of bottles of sparkling water in his hands, and the simple gesture—so sweet, so unexpected—made me laugh.

I took the bottles from him with a smile, placing them on the table, the bubbles inside as effervescent as the energy between us. But as soon as I turned back to him, the space between us seemed to disappear in an instant. I reached out to give him a hug, feeling his warmth as his arms closed around me, but then everything shifted.

Our eyes met again, and there was a pause—just a breath, a moment when the world seemed to stand still. And then, without thinking, we kissed. The second our lips touched, everything else turn upside down. The soft pressure of his mouth against mine sent a rush of warmth through me, making my skin tingle.

In that kiss, I forgot about everything, even the carefully planned dinner waiting just a few feet away. The food, the table, the candles—all of it vanished from my minds as the kiss deepened, pulling us both under. My hands slid up to his shoulders, his grip tightening around my waist, and I felt myself melting into him, lost in the sensation of his touch, the softness of his lips, the way our breaths mingled as we lost ourselves in the moment.

Time seemed to blur. All the anticipation of the day, the careful planning, the excitement—none of it compared to this. There was only the heat between us, the feel of his hands on me, the taste of his kiss. Everything else could wait. For now, all that mattered was this—this perfect, stolen moment, where nothing else existed but us.

The kisses grew deeper, more urgent, as we held each other close. The heat between us intensified with every passing second, our soft moans filling the space. It was clear that sitting down to eat was no longer an option. Our hunger for each other was far stronger than anything waiting on the table. Our hands moved without hesitation, sliding over clothes and skin, undressing each other.

His hands were gentle yet firm, his touch setting my skin alight as my clothes fell away. When we were finally bare, his fingers brushed against me, and a soft, guttural moan escaped his lips as he touch my wet pussy and realised just how ready I was. The warmth between us felt electric, charged with all the desire I had been feeling since I had started preparing for this night. The fantasies that had danced in my mind, imagining this very moment, came rushing back in full force.

We made our way to the bed, our bodies pressing against each other, the heat of our skin meeting in waves. I could feel the tension building inside me, the ache, the need, growing stronger by the second. I wanted him—needed him—with a depth I could barely control. As he hovered over me, I gasped softly, feeling the head of his cock press against my pussy, teasing my clit with slow, deliberate movements.

He moved with a kind of patience that was maddening and exquisite all at once, his body pressing into mine with care, and I felt every nerve, every muscle, responding to him. Each slow push of his cock inside stretched me, filling me completely, until I could feel nothing but the heat of him, the way our bodies came together so perfectly. Our eyes locked, and the intensity of the moment deepened as he leant down, capturing my lips in another slow, lingering kiss.

In that kiss, there was everything—desire, longing, and the deep connection that had been building between us. Our movements were slow, sensual, and unhurried, savouring every second, every touch. The world outside faded into nothing as we lost ourselves in each other, the rest of the night ahead full of nothing but the promise of us.

Our bodies were slick with heat, the tension between us building like a fire neither of us could control. I felt the power in the moment, the energy shifting between us as the air thickened with sweat and desire. He was in my space now—my cage, my rules. Every breath, every movement, seemed charged with a shared understanding that tonight, I would take control.

I wrapped my legs tightly around his, feeling the strength in his body beneath me. In one swift, calculated movement, with a gentle push from him, I managed to turn us both, rolling smoothly until I was on top. Triumph surged through me as I pinned his hands to the bed, feeling his pulse beneath my fingers.

We both smiled, our faces glowing with the thrill of the moment. I could see in his eyes that he knew what I wanted, and with a mixture of excitement and surrender, he whispered, "Yes, babe."

I paused for a moment. "Babe?" I thought, my smile fading ever so slightly. He could have called me by my name, something personal, intimate, even wild. But *babe* felt so ordinary, so common, like it could have been anyone in that bed with him. The frustration simmered beneath the surface, but rather than pulling me out of the moment, it only fuelled my desire. I pressed my hips down harder against him, riding him with newfound intensity, letting my anger blend with the passion between us.

I could feel the heat rise as I moved, the friction igniting every nerve in my body. My hands still holding his wrists down, I shifted slightly, pressing my chest against his, my breath mingling with his as I leant forward. The sensation was overwhelming—my clit rubbing against him, the pulse of my own body in time with his, building and building. His chest rose and fell beneath me, his eyes locked onto mine, both of us lost in the pleasure that was consuming us.

The first wave of release began to ripple through me, slow and unstoppable. My muscles tightened, and I could feel the blood rushing through my veins, every inch of me alive with the sensation of him inside me. I couldn't hold back—the pleasure surged as I moaned, breathless, whispering that I was coming. His hands gripped my hips hard, anchoring me to him as I let myself go, the orgasm washing over me in hot, pulsing waves.

I collapsed forward, my body melting against his, and his lips found my neck, soft and tender, in stark contrast to the fire between us. Before I could catch my breath, he moved, gently shifting me onto my back, sliding between my legs as he filled me once more. There was no pause, no moment to recover—just the pure, relentless drive of his body against mine. The sensation was overwhelming, the pleasure almost too much to bear.

We kissed deeply, our mouths seeking each other as his rhythm slowed, teasing, drawing out the moment. Then, without warning, he pulled out. My body ached with the sudden emptiness, but before I could even draw a full breath, his mouth was on my pussy.

He kissed me there with the same hunger, the same passion, as if he couldn't get enough. His lips moved over me with expert precision, the way he had kissed my mouth, slow and deliberate, making every second feel electric. I gasped, my head falling back as I arched towards him, unable to keep still. My clit was so sensitive, so hard, that every stroke of his tongue sent jolts of pleasure through my entire body.

I lifted my head, needing to see him, needing to watch as he brought me to the brink once again. The sight of him between my legs, his mouth worshiping me with such intensity, made my body tremble. He knew exactly what I wanted, exactly what I needed, and he gave it to me without hesitation.

The second orgasm tore through me, even more powerful than the first. My body convulsed, my hands gripping the sheets as I cried out, lost in the wild, unbridled pleasure. He didn't stop, didn't let up, and as I came in his mouth, we were like animals, consumed by our desire, lost in the rhythm of each other's bodies.

Afterward, we collapsed into each other, our bodies warm and slick with sweat, hearts still pounding. I laughed softly, out of breath, and reached for the bottles of sparkling water on the bedside table. "I need a break from that animal," I teased, playfully swatting at him as he propped himself up on one elbow. He chuckled, his eyes still dark with desire but now softened with amusement.

We drank quietly, the cold water cooling our heated skin, the refreshing taste slipping down our throats like a sweet relief after the wild intensity of the moment. I took a moment to admire him—his chest rising and falling, the beads of sweat still glistening on his skin, his lips curved into a knowing smile, hiding by his beard that I love to touch and fell in my skin.

"How can you keep going?" I wondered aloud, shaking my head in disbelief.

He just grinned, his gaze holding mine in a way that made my stomach flip. "I could ask you the same," he replied, the deep timbre of his voice sending shivers down my spine.

As we sipped our water, our laughter echoed around the room, both of us amazed at how powerless we had been to resist each other. Even the short pause seemed like too much separation. It wasn't long before the tension began to build again, like an electric charge hanging in the air between us. The moment was fragile, held together by our shared glances and the way our bodies still buzzed with unspent energy.

I felt it stirring in me once more—the hunger, the irresistible pull. The water bottles were quickly forgotten, set aside as we found ourselves drawn back together, unable to keep our hands off each other. This time, it was my turn. I kissed him deeply, tasting the lingering sweetness of the water on his lips, my hands sliding down his body as I moved lower, feeling the heat of his skin against mine.

I took his cock in my mouth slowly, enjoying the feel of him, the weight and warmth, as I let him slide deeper. I wanted to drive him wild, to hear him lose himself in the sensation. The taste of his skin filled my senses as I moved rhythmically, my hands and mouth working in unison, teasing, caressing, my lips gliding down the length of him. His groans grew deeper, vibrating through my body, each sound spurring me on as I pushed him further, wanting him to feel every inch of my desire.

When I took him all the way, I felt his muscles tense, his hands gripping the sheets as he moaned low, his voice thick with need. I sucked harder, tasting the salt of his skin, relishing the sound of his gasps as I licked and teased, my hands roaming over his thighs, tracing the hard lines of his body. I could feel his pleasure building, the tension radiating from him in waves, and I knew he was close.

Suddenly, his hands were on me, pulling me up, his mouth capturing mine in a kiss that was both desperate and sweet. He tasted himself on my lips, just as I often tasted myself when he kissed me after going down on me. The sensation was intoxicating—his lips on mine, his tongue exploring my mouth as if to taste the mingling of our desire. I was lost in the kiss, dizzy from the heady combination of passion and connection.

But I wasn't done yet. I needed more. I needed to be in control, to feel him beneath me. With a slow, deliberate movement, I pushed him back onto the bed, straddling him as I guided him inside me once more. I gasped as he filled me, my hips sinking down onto him, the sensation overwhelming as I pressed my hands against his chest. His breath hitched, his eyes locking onto mine with a fire that matched my own.

This time, though, I remembered the *babe* he had whispered earlier, and a sly smile spread across my face. I wanted him to call me by my name, to know exactly who was with him in that moment. I place one of my hands around his neck, I whispered, "What's my name?"

His eyes widened, surprise flickering across his face as I tightened my grip, my hand pressing into his neck with authority. "What is my name?" I repeated, my voice soft but dripping with power. He hesitated for a moment, and then his expression changed—desire and surrender mingling in his gaze as he answered in a husky whisper, "Gatinha."

The sound of it sent a thrill through me, and I knew then that he was completely mine in that moment. I smiled wickedly, feeling the rush of control as I began to move my hips, riding him with a newfound intensity. My hands slid up to his neck, lightly pressing, and his eyes fluttered shut as the pressure brought us both to the edge of something even deeper. The way he responded made me feel like I had unleashed something primal in him, and in myself.

With a sudden surge of energy, he flipped me over, his strength pinning me beneath him as he lifted me into position. My heart raced with anticipation, and I felt the wildness in the air, the raw passion taking over. He turned me onto my knees, pulling my hips up as he positioned himself behind me. My breath caught in my throat as he entered me, his thrusts slow at first, deliberate, letting me feel every inch of him filling me.

The sounds of our bodies moving together echoed in the room—the slap of skin, the soft moans, the rhythmic creak of the bed. I pushed back against him, wanting more, needing more. The pleasure was almost unbearable, every nerve in my body ignited as I turned my head, my hair falling over my face, to catch a glimpse of him behind me. The sight of him—his eyes dark with lust, his jaw clenched, his body taut with the effort to hold himself back—made my heart race even faster.

He pressed my face into the bed, pushing harder, urging him on with my movements. "Harder," I whispered, the words barely audible through the sounds of our shared pleasure. And he did—his pace quickened, his hands gripping my hips as he drove deeper, the intensity of it making my body tremble.

In a desperate attempt to push us both over the edge, I stretched one hand back, managing to grab his balls. His response was immediate—he moaned loud, his voice raw and animalistic as he gasped, "Yes, grab my balls." The feeling of him pulsing inside me, combined with the grip of my hand, sent us both spiralling into something animal and uncontrollable.

I felt the orgasm building in me, powerful and unstoppable, like a force of nature taking over. I screamed his name, my voice cracking with the intensity of the pleasure, my entire body shaking as I came, hard. I was lost in the sensation, every muscle in my body tightening and then releasing in one explosive, breathtaking moment.

He was right behind me, the sound of his moans filling the room as we both let go, lost in each other, in the heat, in the sheer, wild abandon of the moment. And for a second, I felt like I was someone else entirely, transformed by the passion, the connection, the pure, raw desire between us.

The orgasm tore through me like a storm, violent and unrelenting. My body shook, every nerve ignited as the pleasure exploded within me. It felt as though something deep inside me snapped, releasing the animal I had been holding back. My muscles tensed, every bone in my body seemingly cracking under the pressure, and in that moment, I felt feral—like a black panther, wild and free, prowling in the night.

I growled softly, my breath ragged, my body vibrating with the power of the moment. I was no longer just myself—I had become something primal, something untamed. My hair fell wild across my face, my eyes sharp and focused as I looked back at him.

And then, I saw him. His eyes locked onto mine, dark and intense, like a beast staring down its prey. His chest heaved with exertion, his body glistening with sweat, and the hunger in his gaze was undeniable. He looked at me not as a lover, but as something wild, raw, and powerful that neither of us could control.

For a moment, we were no longer just two people lost in passion. We were animals, creatures of instinct, driven by the wild forces inside us that had finally been unleashed. And in that moment, as I felt the panther rise within me and saw the beast in his eyes, I knew that we had both crossed a line, venturing into something far beyond the ordinary. We were lost to the wild, to each other, and there was no going back.

Chapter 29
Time Out Diner Time

Back in the warmth of reality, we both finally tumble out of bed, breathless and flushed, with laughter still dancing on our lips. It's time for dinner—though by now, the food has cooled, and the once-perfect salmon is undoubtedly dry. We exchange a glance and burst into laughter, the kind that only comes when everything has gone so deliciously off script, but it doesn't matter. His presence makes everything else irrelevant.

He's so polite, so caring, that even though the meal isn't as I'd hoped, his words are soft, reassuring. "It looks amazing," he says with a genuine smile, "even after we got a little… distracted." His easy-going nature instantly relaxes me, making me feel like we'd done everything just right.

I bring the food to the table, the candles still flickering softly, casting a warm glow around us. As I set the plates down, I catch the way his eyes soften, full of something I can't quite name but that sends a rush of warmth through my chest. He doesn't say much, but the look on his face says it all—he's touched by the effort, by the care I've put into this night. It fills me with happiness just watching him, feeling his appreciation without needing words.

We sit together, placing food on each other's plates, and I watch eagerly as he takes his first bite of the prawns. His face lights up in pure delight, his eyes widening in surprise at how much he enjoys them. "These are perfect," he says between bites, his voice full of genuine pleasure, and I can't help but beam with pride. Seeing that gorgeous, happy face as he savours each bite fills my heart with warmth. I hadn't realised how much joy I'd get from watching him enjoy something I made with my own hands.

We move on to the salmon, and I know it's a bit dry, but he doesn't miss a beat. "Still so good," he says, his compliments never wavering, and I know he means it. He's making sure I feel good about the meal, and I can see it in his eyes that he truly appreciates everything. It makes me laugh softly, knowing that even though the food wasn't perfect, the night still feels magical because we've made it ours.

We giggle through the rest of the meal, sharing little jokes and stolen glances across the table, the atmosphere light and filled with easy joy. When I bring out dessert, I tease him to save room, knowing I'm not the biggest fan of sweets, but I can't resist having a little with him. His reaction to the yogurt and berries is priceless—he lights up like a kid getting his favourite toy, his face full of excitement. "This is amazing!" he exclaims, and I can't help but smile at how happy he is, his enthusiasm infectious as we finish the meal, full and content.

Once the plates are cleared and the candles burn a little lower, it doesn't take long for us to find our way back to each other. We can't stay apart for long. As soon as we stand, we're pulled into another embrace, laughter turning into soft sighs as we kiss again, and just like that, we're back in bed, the music playing softly in the background as we lose ourselves in each other once more. It feels like we're dancing to a song only we can hear, moving in perfect rhythm as the heat between us builds all over again.

We kiss and touch, letting the night carry us away as we enjoy each other's bodies, the connection between us deepening with every passing moment. And when he makes me come again, my body trembling beneath his touch, I know this night is one I'll never forget.

But eventually, the night begins to wind down. He gets dressed slowly, his movements reluctant, as though neither of us really wants the night to end. Part of me wishes I could ask him to stay, to fall asleep beside me and wake up in each other's arms again, like we did on our second dinner date. There's something different about tonight, something more intimate, more connected, and waking up with him now would feel like the next step. But I don't stop him.

He leaves quietly, with a soft kiss and a lingering touch, and though I wish for a moment that he would stay, I know it's not quite time yet. We'll get there. The night may be over, but the connection between us has grown, and I fall asleep with the sweetest smile.

Chapter 30
The Symbol of Eight

Lately, everything in my life had started falling into place, almost effortlessly, as if the universe itself was whispering a new harmony into my soul. But something else had begun to catch my attention—something small, yet persistent.

I had been seeing the number eight everywhere. At first, I brushed it off as coincidence. But day after day, the number appeared—in the times on my phone, the pages of books, even in the way shadows played on the pavement. I couldn't shake the feeling that it meant something. My curiosity eventually got the better of me, and I started to explore its significance in numerology.

It turns out, the number eight holds powerful spiritual meaning—representing balance, the harmony between material success and spiritual growth. It also symbolises infinity, an endless flow of energy. The more I read, the more I felt it aligned with my current journey. I had been searching for that balance, trying to reconcile my ambitions with something deeper. It felt like the universe was guiding me, though toward what, I wasn't quite sure yet.

Then, there was Gato. He was successful, grounded, and constantly encouraging me to pursue my dreams. But there was one problem—I wasn't entirely sure what those dreams were. I knew I wanted to help people, and mental health had always intrigued me, but when it came to picking a specific path, I felt adrift. *Should I work with adults, couples, or families? Should I focus on trauma, anxiety, or something else entirely?* There were so many possibilities, yet none felt quite right.

Our connection, though new, felt significant. I used to joke with myself that while I was mentally picking out wedding venues, Gato was still deciding where we should have our next dinner. He hadn't caught on yet to the depth of what I saw between us, but I figured that was okay. Eventually, he'd see it, too. I was in no rush.

Even as I wrestled with uncertainty in my career, Gato's presence made the process less daunting. His steady belief in me was reassuring. I didn't know exactly what path I would take but having him by my side gave me the courage to keep moving forward.

The 3 A.M. Vision

Then came the turning point.

It was around 3 a.m.—the hour when the world is utterly still, and time feels suspended. I woke up suddenly, unusually alert. As I opened my eyes, I found myself staring at the ceiling of my flat. And that's when it happened—the vision.

It was as if shapes, words, and light were writing themselves across the ceiling, illuminating the darkness around me. The message was undeniable, though it took me a moment to process: *Children.* I was meant to help children.

For months, I had been struggling to figure out who I was supposed to serve in the world of mental health. And there, in the stillness of the night, the answer appeared. I could see their faces—children laughing, learning, and growing. I felt their energy, their innocence, and their need for protection and guidance. It was as if the universe had lit up my purpose, writing it out for me to finally see. I was meant to help children navigate the challenges of life and protect their joy, that untainted spark we so often lose as adults.

When the vision faded, I was left with a sense of certainty I hadn't felt in a long time. The answer had been there all along, waiting for me to recognise it.

With this newfound clarity, the path forward became obvious. I wanted to focus on children's mental health—on helping young minds build resilience, develop emotional intelligence, and gain the tools to cope with life's challenges. It wasn't just a career choice anymore; it felt like a calling.

But even with the fire of that vision burning inside me, I still struggled with the practicalities. The first step was updating my CV and starting the job search, but asking for help had always been difficult for me. Therapy and Stoicism had taught me that asking for help wasn't a sign of weakness, yet a part of me still hesitated. But this time, I knew I couldn't do it alone.

Naturally, I thought of Gato.

After making some adjustments to my CV, I nervously sent it to him, unsure of how he'd respond. It was the first time I had asked him for something so personal. Within minutes, my phone rang.

"I'll come over," he said. "We'll work on it together."

Ten minutes later, he was at my door, his calm presence filling my flat. We sat at the table, the soft murmur of the TV playing in the background while he combed through my CV. Outside, it was quiet—the windows faced the back of the building, away from the noise of the street. The world felt still, as if time had slowed down, and all that mattered was the quiet strength he offered me in that moment.

He believed in me—even during the moments when I wasn't entirely sure I believed in myself. And somehow, that belief was all I needed.

As we sat there together, I began to realise that everything was coming full circle. The balance I had been searching for—between love, purpose, and personal growth—was starting to take shape. I could see myself working with children, guiding them through their emotional and mental development, helping them grow into their potential.

The number eight had been my sign all along—a reminder that balance is possible. My love for Gato, my passion for helping children, and my own spiritual growth were all beginning to align. I no longer felt lost. The path was clear now. I just needed to keep moving forward, trusting the universe would guide me the rest of the way.

Chapter 31
Hand in Hand: A Sunday Walk by the River Thames

What a way to spend a Sunday with someone who walked into my life and changed everything—changed the way I saw myself, the way I envisioned the future, the way I understood love, and even the way I allowed myself to receive it. Gato didn't just alter my perspective; he transformed the world around me. Today marks only one month since our first date at the pub, but it feels like I've known him for years. Four weeks, yet somehow, it's as though he's been a part of my life forever.

It's one of those perfect summer days in London, where the sky is a soft blue, the sun casting golden light over the streets, and the city hums with quiet energy. Gato suggests a walk by the Thames, and I agree—it's the kind of day meant for wandering without a plan. I dress simply, casually, but thoughtfully. A pair of skinny jeans, a long-sleeved shirt, and my most comfortable shoes, because I know we'll likely be walking for hours. I take nothing but the essentials: my keys, my phone, and the soft, lingering scent of my favourite perfume, the kind that makes you feel complete. My clothes without it would feel unfinished. I don't mind going without makeup, but never without my scent—it's like leaving the house without a part of myself.

As I step outside, the streets of Hampstead are alive. Cafes are buzzing with families indulging in lazy Sunday brunches, their laughter and clinking cutlery drifting out into the air. The aroma of coffee, freshly baked croissants, and the sweet hint of maple syrup fills the breeze. I walk past them with a smile, feeling light, almost giddy with excitement at the thought of seeing Gato again. *My Gato... Can I call him that yet?* A shy smile tugs at my lips as I make my way to the station.

The tube is quiet as I step inside, though the usual hum of the city is ever-present, a comforting rhythm beneath the surface. Gato had moved out of Hampstead recently, so he's not my neighbour anymore, but Camden Town isn't far. I get a message from him, saying he might be a little late because the station's packed, as it always is on Sundays. I can almost hear his voice in the words—casual and easy-going.

Stepping off the train at Charing Cross, the familiar voice of the announcer echoes through the station: *Mind the gap*. It's something every Londoner and tourist alike can recite without thinking, a piece of the city ingrained in daily life. The station is bustling, as it always is, people weaving in and out, their footsteps a constant beat against the tiles. I take my time, walking slowly, enjoying the moment. Gato's late, so there's no need to hurry. I glance around, trying to orient myself, looking for the stairs to the exit. As I turn left to head up, I feel a light pressure on my back, as though someone is trying to nudge me forward.

Startled, I jump, my heart skipping a beat, ready to confront whoever pushed me. But when I whirl around, I find Gato standing there, grinning like a mischievous kid who's just played the best trick.

"Gato!" I laugh, my surprise melting into a wide smile.

He's dressed casually in his baggy jeans and yellow sweatshirt. It suits him perfectly—relaxed, effortless, as if he's never needed to try to look good. He pulls me into a hug right there, in the middle of the station, his arms wrapping around me in that way that only he can. It's the kind of embrace that squeezes you just right, grounding you, making you feel like everything is exactly where it should be. I've never been one for public displays of affection—always a little too self-conscious—but with Gato, it's different. He's changed me. I don't care who's watching or what they think. In this moment, it's just us.

His lips find mine, soft and familiar, and for a second, the busy station falls away. I can taste the sweetness of his kiss, warm and unhurried, as though time is bending around us. The distant sounds of footsteps and announcements fade into the background. His scent—a mix of clean cotton and something uniquely him—fills my senses.

Finally, we break apart, breathless but laughing, and make our way out of the station, our hands entwined. There's no rush, no plan—just the easy rhythm of being together.

"Let's get some coffee," Gato suggests, his voice light with that familiar hint of warmth.

Before we even make it to the coffee shop, we stop again, unable to resist more kisses, more hugs, as if we've been apart for far too long. His hands are on me, and mine on him, our fingers tracing invisible lines on each other's backs, our laughter bubbling up between kisses. The world spins on, indifferent to our little bubble, but inside it, there's only the two of us.

And in that moment, I realise he's not just changing the way I see things—he's changing the way I feel everything. Every sensation, every sound, every breath feels more vivid, more alive, because of him.

Just before we found a coffee shop, I realised how fast we were walking. Gato led the way, excited, his pace almost pulling me along. I'm used to walking quickly myself, especially when I'm on my own, but lately, I've started slowing down, making a point to enjoy my walks, to take in the world around me instead of rushing through it. But here I was, nearly jogging to keep up with him. I smiled to myself, amused by the thought. *Wow, I've actually met someone who walks faster than me.* I chuckled quietly, trying to focus back on what he was saying as we made our way down the busy street.

Suddenly, he spotted a small coffee shop, its aroma drifting out to mingle with the city air. We stepped inside, the comforting scent of roasted beans wrapping around us like a warm blanket. The hum of conversation and the clatter of cups created a cosy, familiar atmosphere. I ordered my usual—a black Americano, but only half a cup of water. I don't like it full; I'm too clumsy for that. Walking fast with a full cup of hot coffee? A recipe for disaster. Gato ordered his oat latte, his go-to drink.

As I turned to leave the counter, Gato made a quick stop at the sugar station. I watched as he casually scooped some brown sugar into his coffee. I couldn't help but burst out laughing.

"Wait a second, Oh no, sugar in your coffee? I thought you were perfect!" I teased, raising an eyebrow, half in disbelief and half in playful amusement.

He grinned back at me, his eyes sparkling with that familiar, mischievous light. "Yes," he said, with a cheeky smirk, "but it's brown sugar."

I laughed at the absurdity of it, the playful banter so easy between us. In my mind, I kept chuckling. *Brown sugar? Really?* It felt like such a small, silly thing, but it made me feel even closer to him. Just one of those quirks that make you smile.

As we walked out of the café, Gato took a sip of his coffee and immediately frowned.

"Ugh, it's cold," he grumbled, clearly disappointed.

I felt for him—there's nothing worse than expecting a warm, comforting cup of coffee and getting a lukewarm mess instead. Cold coffee is only acceptable when it's iced, and even then, it's a choice.

"I'm so sorry," I said, giving him a sympathetic look and pulling him in for a hug. My arms wrapped around him, hoping to ease the frustration, even if just a little. "That's the worst." He sighed but smiled, leaning into the embrace for a moment before we continued walking.

He wanted to show me a building he liked, something that had caught his eye on one of his walks. Since we didn't have a set destination in mind, just a loose plan to wander through the city and along the Thames, I was happy to let him lead the way. It felt good not to have a rigid schedule, to simply walk and talk, taking in the city and each other.

We finally reached the building Gato had been talking about—a new development right by the river, sleek and modern, still under construction. I could already see how beautiful it would be when it was finished, set against the backdrop of London's timeless charm. This city, my second home, never ceased to amaze me. London's ever-evolving beauty was all around us, and as I listened to Gato talk about the building, pointing out details with that unmistakable excitement in his voice, I felt a wave of gratitude wash over me. "Thank you, God," I whispered in my mind, feeling so lucky to be here, walking these streets with him. Gato, my perfect tour guide, showing me his world.

We stood there for a few moments, taking it all in—the building and the life surrounding us. And then, as if drawn by some invisible force, we made our way down to the river. The second we reached the edge of the Thames, the magic of the moment took over. Gato wrapped his arm around my waist, pulling me close, and kissed me deeply. My body melted into him, everything else fading away. The view, the scene, the summer air, his touch—it was one of those perfect moments in life you wish could last forever.

After our brief stop for kisses, we continued across Waterloo Bridge, heading toward Southbank Centre's food market. The view from the bridge was breathtaking, London laid out in all its summer glory. The city was alive—music for our eyes, as if every street and building pulsed with good energy. People everywhere, happy faces glowing in the sun, a sense of freedom filling the air. But honestly, I wasn't paying attention to any of it. All I could see was Gato. The way he talked, his voice with that accent that melted me every time, the way he smiled, his beard that I had this constant urge to rub with my fingers. He was everything in that moment. I felt like a teenager, completely swept up in her crush. And yes, I had a "big" crush on him.

When we finally arrived at the market, it was packed. The scent of food filled the air—Caribbean dishes spiced with fiery chilies, Chinese stir-fries, Japanese sushi, and, of course, Italian food. Gato, the food lover that he is, immediately got excited. He stopped in front of an Italian stall, gesturing toward the bruschetta, his eyes lighting up as he told me how much he loved it. But not today—he had a craving. "Guess what I want?" he asked, grinning. When he stopped in front of a burger stall, I couldn't help but laugh. *A burger?* I hadn't expected that, but the spontaneity of it was fun. Why not? Sometimes, it's good to throw caution to the wind and indulge.

When I told him I'd have a burger too, his face changed. He didn't seem pleased with the idea of me having just any burger. His expression became thoughtful, almost worried, as he started considering where to take me. He wanted me to have the best burger, not just any random market stall burger. I could see his mind working, searching for the perfect place. I tried to tell him it didn't matter—that I was happy to have whatever—but he wasn't listening. Determined to find something better, he suggested Borough Market. I laughed, not wanting to go that far, but it was clear he was on a mission.

As we wandered past a restaurant, the wind began to pick up, the air turning a bit chilly. Without a second thought, we ducked inside. I didn't care too much about the food at that point—I just wanted to be with him. The place had a great vibe—families filling the tables, and the sound of rock and roll from the '60s and '70s playing softly in the background. It felt cosy and familiar, the perfect spot to warm up.

Looking for a seat, Gato insisted on sitting right next to me. I wasn't going to argue—after all, I wanted to be right next to him too. As soon as we sat down, he wrapped his arm around me, squeezing me tightly like he always did, making me feel like the happiest person in the world. He kept squeezing me, and I kept smiling, loving every second of it. His squeezes felt like his way of saying "I'm here, and I'm not letting go." And I wouldn't have it any other way.

We glanced at the menu, and I ordered a simple cheeseburger and fries. Gato, on the other hand, went all out, choosing the biggest burger with all the toppings. We both smiled at each other, excitement written all over our faces. There was an undeniable joy between us, the kind that radiated so clearly that anyone nearby could see it. We were like two lovebirds, just discovering each other, wrapped up in the magic of the moment.

As we waited for our food, I couldn't help but steal glances at him—lost in the moment, completely captivated by his presence. And then, out of nowhere, Gato started to sing. His voice, soft and unguarded, rose above the murmur of the restaurant, matching the rock and roll song playing in the background. I felt my heart skip a beat.

There he was, singing to me, and in that moment, and there I was in love. I couldn't believe what my eyes were seeing or what my heart was feeling. It was magic, pure and simple. How could I have imagined that I would ever be sitting here with someone who would sing just for me? I had dreamt of moments like this, imagined them in the quiet of my mind, but I never truly believed they would happen. And yet, here he was—effortlessly making my dream a reality.

His voice wrapped around me, a melody I never wanted to end. As he sang, his eyes sparkled with that playful glint I adored, and I found myself completely enchanted by him. He was so carefree, so full of life and warmth, that it made everything else fade away. The world beyond us ceased to exist. It was just him and me, caught in this perfect bubble of time.

He smiled as he sang, his face lighting up with every word, as though the song was meant just for us. His hands finding mine, and the warmth of his touch sent a wave of electricity through me. We sat there, facing each other, his voice carrying us both into this moment of pure bliss. I couldn't stop smiling—couldn't stop feeling like the luckiest person in the world to have found someone like him.

As his fingers gently squeezed mine, I realised how perfect everything felt. I had always been drawn to him, but now, in this moment, I felt myself falling deeper, sinking into the love that was growing in me. The way he moved, the way he smiled as he sang, the way his whole face lit up—it all made me feel like I was living a dream.

Just as I thought the moment couldn't be any more perfect, we were interrupted by the soft clearing of a throat. The waitress had arrived, holding our plates—our burgers, steaming and ready. Gato stopped singing. I laughed softly, the spell not quite broken, but gently set aside. As the waitress placed our food down, Gato smiled at me as if to say, "Let's kill it."

Even as we prepared to dig into our burgers, I noticed something wasn't quite right. There were more toppings on mine than I had asked for—pickles, onions, maybe even some extra sauce I hadn't wanted. I hesitated, glancing over at Gato.

He had already taken a big, satisfied bite out of his burger, his face lighting up with that unmistakable look of contentment. He was enjoying every bite, and here I was, debating whether or not to make a fuss.

I started with the fries, picking at them absentmindedly as I weighed my options. *Should I tell him? Should I call the waitress over and ask for the right burger?* My mind raced with the possibilities. But then, I looked at Gato again—so happy, so immersed in the moment—and I couldn't bring myself to interrupt that. If I asked for a new burger, it would mean waiting while he ate alone, and that felt like it would spoil the moment we were sharing. The last thing I wanted was to create some unnecessary tension over a few extra toppings.

So I decided. It's just a burger, I thought. *Burger is burger, right?* And besides, it's not like I was a huge burger enthusiast anyway. I gave a small, tentative bite. The flavours were different from what I expected, but not bad at all. In fact, the longer I chewed, the more I realised it didn't really matter. What mattered was being there with him, sharing this experience.

With our bellies full, it was the perfect time to stretch our legs and explore more of the city. Gato, ever the confident guide, knew exactly where to take us next. We wandered through the streets, eventually making our way to Soho. Seeing Soho through his eyes was something else entirely—every road, every corner was a story waiting to be told. I'd passed through these streets countless times, but never like this.

We strolled down Denmark Street, a place I'd always walked by without a second thought. But today, it was different. Gato's voice filled the air as he painted pictures with his words, bringing the street to life in ways I'd never imagined. He told me of its rich history, a street steeped in the stories of legendary musicians, the birthplace of so many rock and roll dreams. It carried his memories, too—moments he'd lived and breathed as someone who loved music just as much as the greats who once walked these streets.

We passed by the old guitar shops, their windows filled with beautiful instruments, each one seeming to hum with untold stories. The guitars stood like relics from another time, their strings vibrating with the energy of the music that had echoed down this street for decades. The magic of the place became real to me, as if lyrics hung in the air, waiting to be plucked by the next passing musician. I could feel the heartbeat of rock and roll here, and for the first time, I understood why people who loved this music held Denmark Street in such high regard.

Gato spoke with such passion, sharing stories of the famous artists who had once called this street their own, and their spirits still lingering in the air. His voice was rich with knowledge, his brain a treasure trove of memories and facts. I found myself growing more and more fascinated with each word, not just by the stories themselves, but by him. The way his mind worked, the way he could turn an ordinary street into something extraordinary—it was captivating. I had always loved the minds of people who could think deeply, who could tell stories and weave them into something greater. And here Gato was, doing exactly that.

As we moved past the road, he suddenly mentioned the famous graffiti artist Banksy. I had not heard the name before, of course, but Gato's eyes lit up as he began to tell me about him. The way he described Banksy's art was mesmerising—the blend of satire and political commentary, the way his pieces were both bold and subtle, daring yet fleeting. Gato spoke about the mysterious artist as though he were an old friend, someone whose work had touched him in a personal way. I listened intently, hanging on to every word as Gato recounted the history of Banksy's rise to fame, the artist who challenged the very idea of what art could be and where it could exist.

Just as we were wrapped up in our conversation, we stumbled upon a small shop, its windows adorned with Banksy's iconic art. There was a little exhibition happening inside, and without a second thought, we stepped in. The moment we entered, I was surrounded by Banksy's world—his famous pieces on display, from the stencilled girl with a balloon, floating away in the wind, to the riot police with smiley faces, each one a striking commentary on society. The space was filled with Banksy's signature dark humour, his clever subversion of political and social norms, and I could see why Gato was so drawn to his work.

The shop was filled with more than just art; it had become a sanctuary for Banksy's ideas. Souvenirs of every kind lined the shelves—T-shirts with his iconic designs. It was a fascinating place, and Gato moved through it with such enthusiasm, pointing out his favourite pieces and sharing little-known facts about each one. His excitement was infectious, and I found myself grinning as we wandered through the small exhibition, taking in the art, the commentary, and the energy of it all.

It was the perfect way to end our impromptu city tour—a blend of history, art, and stories that made me see the city in a completely new light. Gato had shown me a side of London I hadn't known existed, and I loved every second of it.

As we stepped back out into the street, the evening air was cooler now, and the streets around us were alive with people enjoying the last light of day. We kept walking, talking about everything and nothing, wrapped up in each other and the energy of the city. There was no rush to get anywhere; the whole day had felt like a perfect flow of moments, one leading naturally to the next.

Eventually, without saying much, we decided to head back to my place. We get in a taxi and there was a quiet understanding between us, a knowing smile that passed between our eyes. Gato leant in, brushing his lips against mine softly, and in that moment, the world around us fell away. As he always says, "It just starts with a kiss." And with that, we walked into my place, ready to let whatever happened next unfold in its own time.

Chapter 32
The Pink Candle Holder and the Number Eight

My morning reflections had become the cornerstone of my routine. As I walked towards Primrose Hill, I let my mind settle into a meditative state, opening myself to the lessons hidden within the events of my life. Each step I took was a grounding experience, drawing me closer to a sense of clarity. The cool morning air was crisp against my skin, awakening me to the day, while the soft rustling of leaves underfoot added rhythm to my thoughts. It was during these moments that I found balance, even when life was far from perfect.

I had learnt to embrace the idea that I'm just a simple mortal—imperfect and ever-evolving. But I couldn't deny that life had become a little easier since I started practicing mindfulness. The world didn't seem so overwhelming when I met it with a calm mind.

The best way to kickstart my day was to complete my workout. The gym had always been my refuge, a place where the outside world faded away, leaving only the focus of my own physical and emotional strength. That day, the Body Pump class was packed—people were buzzing with energy, ready to push their limits over the next 45 minutes.

As the instructor's voice echoed through the room, I caught my reflection in the mirror. I felt powerful, my muscles contracting with each rep, my body moving with discipline and precision. This was the moment I felt most in control, most alive. The weights in my hands grounded me, yet I felt like I could conquer anything. The rhythmic clanging of barbells and the synchronised movements of everyone around me created a collective pulse of energy, as if we were all drawing strength from one another.

By the end of the session, I was drenched in sweat, but the surge of dopamine rushing through my veins left me euphoric. As I headed to the changing room, I briefly considered treating myself to the sauna, but realised I had forgotten my flip-flops and swimsuit. No matter—I didn't care about the mess of my sweaty hair or the flushed face staring back at me. I felt beautiful, radiating an energy that made me glow from within.

It didn't hurt that I had a handsome Englishman who reminded me of that every day. Gato's words of affirmation stirred something deep inside me. His compliments felt like more than just words—they made me believe in my own beauty. Love had that effect. When you're in love, everything takes on a softer glow, and suddenly the world seems more beautiful, filled with endless possibility.

Leaving the gym, still basking in the afterglow of the workout, a corner shop caught my attention. I wasn't in any hurry to get home, so I decided to pop in and have a look. It was one of those quaint little shops that specialised in home décor, the kind that felt like a treasure hunt as you walked through it. The air inside was warm and inviting, scented with vanilla and sandalwood candles, mingling with the faint earthy smell of wooden furniture on display.

I had always loved browsing for home décor, constantly picturing how my dream home would look. Strangely enough, I never dreamt of a massive house—just one of good size, with a cosy garden and a round entrance. The front door would be at the centre, framed by blooming flowers and red stone walls. Inside, the hall would be soft and inviting, painted in shades of white and beige, leading to an open kitchen where the morning light would stream through large windows overlooking the garden.

In my vision, I could see myself preparing breakfast for Gato and me, with soft music playing in the background. The smell of fresh eggs sizzling in the pan and the rich aroma of coffee filling the room as I moved effortlessly through the kitchen. I imagined Gato coming up behind me, wrapping his arms around me in what we jokingly called a "squeeze," and kissing my neck, whispering about his plans for the day ahead. It was a simple, beautiful life—the kind of life I could already feel in my bones, even though it hadn't fully materialized yet.

Lost in thoughts of my dream home, I meandered through the shop, fingers grazing the delicate textures of linen throws and rustic ceramics. That's when something at the back of the shop caught my eye—a candle holder, tucked away in a quiet corner. But not just any candle. It was shaped like the number eight, and it stopped me in my tracks.

The number eight had been appearing in my life recently, almost hauntingly so. And now here it was again, this time in the form of a pink candle—the exact colour I had worn on New Year's Eve. I had chosen pink that night because someone once told me it brought love into your life. And I suppose they were right. Because here I was, deeply in love, with Gato beside me.

I reached for the candle holder, my fingers trembling slightly as I picked it up. It felt like more than just wax and wick. It was a symbol—a reminder of the balance I had been seeking, of the harmony between the spiritual and the material. It also felt like a sign from the universe, assuring me that I was on the right path, that love, and purpose were intertwined, guiding me forward.

Without a second thought, I bought the candle and left the shop, feeling a sense of joy and gratitude that I couldn't contain. As I walked home, the crisp air filled my lungs, and the soft hum of the city felt distant, almost like background music to the symphony playing in my heart. I couldn't wait to get home and light the candle, to thank the universe for the abundance in my life—for the love I had found, the clarity in my purpose, the roof over my head, my family, and most of all, for Gato.

The moment I stepped through my door, I wasted no time. I lit a candle as a small act of reverence. Its flame flickered gently in the dim light of my flat, casting soft shadows on the walls. I stood there for a moment, my heart full, and whispered a quiet thank you. Thank you for the life I had rebuilt. Thank you for the happiness that now filled my days. Thank you for the people I loved, for the love I had found in Gato.

I closed my eyes, inhaling deeply, feeling gratitude wash over me. The number eight had brought me here, to this place of balance and contentment. It wasn't just a number anymore—it was a symbol of everything I had been working towards. And in that moment, with the candle's soft glow lighting up the room, I knew I was exactly where I was meant to be.

Chapter 33
Inspired by Love the Magic of Loves' Words

31st of August. So much has happened in just a few weeks, and it feels like I've become a completely different person. Love has a way of doing that—turning your world upside down and changing everything, sometimes before you even realise it. All I want now is to love and show love, not just to Gato, but to everyone around me. It's as if my heart has opened wider than I ever thought possible. Since my mother left home, I've had to find ways to fill my spare time.

I still have a month until university starts, and I haven't found a job in the field I want for my new career, which only deepens my restlessness. I'm not the type to sit still and wait for life to happen. I need to feel like I'm doing something, like I'm creating, producing, becoming. Maybe that's why I've thrown myself into the gym, burning energy to make time pass, but physical activity only gets me so far.

One morning, as I sip my coffee and look out the window of my flat, reflecting on everything that's changed, two clear visions flash in my mind. The first comes in the form of my inner voice, louder and clearer than usual: *Why don't you write a book about your 'Awakening'?* The thought stuns me at first. I've never considered myself a writer, but the idea fills me with excitement. What happened to me over these past months has been nothing short of a spiritual rebirth. I spoke to God, and He answered me, not with words but with signals, through people, through the universe itself. How could I keep that to myself? It's not just my story—it's a story that might help someone out there, someone who's lost or searching for the same answers I was.

But then reality hits me like a jolt, as it always does. *I'm not a writer.* The thought is sharp, almost mocking. *How could I write a book?* Doubts start crowding my mind, whispering all the reasons why I'm not good enough. Then, that inner voice, stronger now, seems to shout at me: "Just do it!" And so, I follow the call, hands trembling as I open my laptop and stare at the blank page. The first few paragraphs are terrible. The words stumble out clumsily, not at all like the thoughts and emotions flowing freely in my mind.

My fingers are slow, but my thoughts are wild, untamed. I pause, frustrated, and then I realise—I need to organise my mind before I try to capture it on the page.

I've always been a structured person, someone who needs lists, plans, and clarity. So, I start making notes. I brainstorm, writing down fragments of memories, flashes of emotion, moments that defined me. And suddenly, something shifts. The ideas begin to flow in a way that feels natural. I'm not just typing words anymore; I'm pouring out pieces of myself. My heart, my soul, my experiences, they all find a home on the page. Here I am now, sharing my love life and my spiritual awakening, baring everything with a strange sense of freedom.

As my fingers fly across the keyboard, I laugh at myself. "How did I not know I could do this?" I've always loved the arts—reading, drawing, music, dance—they were all a part of my life from the very beginning. As a child, I loved to draw and dance, dreaming of being famous one day, of making my mark on the world. I was always the one creating something, always using my hands to craft little pieces of magic. And now, my hands are doing something truly special—writing my own book, telling my own story.

This isn't just about me anymore. It's as if I've been called for something much bigger than I ever imagined. This time, it's not just for my family—it's for the entire world. Life is not about what you lost, it's about what you discover along the way. It's about understanding that you can always start over, that it's never too late to make your dreams come true, and most importantly, to love yourself and the life you've been given.

And maybe, just maybe, I'm dreaming too big again. I always dream big, wanting too much. But what if this story becomes something more? I can't help but fantasise about it, imagining my book turning into a movie, seeing actors playing Gato and me on the big screen. Names of actors float into my mind, and the thought makes me smile. The sheer joy of it, the feeling of fulfilment, spreads through my body, lifting me high as if I'm flying into the universe with every word I write.

Writing has become the best way to express all these feelings inside me—the good, the bad, the uncertain. It's more than just a way to pass the time while the universe works its magic. Writing helps me process the doubts and fears, especially about Gato. With every word, I push away the negative thoughts and reaffirm my faith in the process, in love, in life. But the doubts about Gato—they rise with the intensity of my feelings for him, pulling me deeper into the unknown. I'm falling harder than I ever imagined, and it scares me. I can't deny that. There's so much uncertainty, but at the same time, something bigger is brewing. I can feel it, like a shift in the air, a signal from the universe that my life is about to change in ways I can't even comprehend yet.

So, I tell myself to let go. To leave the future in God's hands and focus on the present. That's the only way to make sure my dreams become a reality. As for Gato—this handsome Englishman who's been driving this Brazilian woman crazy in love—I'll take it one day at a time. No matter what happens next, I know that love, in all its magical, maddening forms, is shaping me into exactly who I'm meant to be.

Chapter 34
Whispers of the Dawn

3.53 a.m. Eyes wide open. I lie there, staring at the dark ceiling, knowing full well that no matter how hard I try, sleep won't return. It never does at this hour. I've learnt to surrender to it, especially when the clock edges close to 4 a.m. It's not ideal, but it's better than the dreaded pre-3 a.m. wakings. I sigh and get out of bed. Maybe it's time to seek help for this insomnia, but that's a thought for later. Right now, the night calls for coffee. The quiet hum of my kettle fills the stillness of the room as I fumble around the kitchen.

As the coffee brews, the soft, familiar gurgle of water rising to a boil, I glance at my phone. No message from Gato. It's Tuesday morning, and he always texts goodnight when he gets home from work. But last night, there was nothing. A slight twinge of unease flickers through my mind. It's not something he "has" to do, of course. I have no control over that. I just hope he's okay.

The darkness outside is thick, mysterious—the kind that feels alive. The world beyond my window is blanketed in silence, as if the universe itself is holding its breath. I gaze into it, say a small prayer, then turn back to the glowing screen of my laptop.

There he is—Gato. A goofy selfie he sent me over the weekend, his smile wide and playful. I'd loved it so much that I made it my wallpaper. His face greets me now, full of light, and despite the quiet worry gnawing at the back of my mind, a smile breaks across my own face. "Good morning," I whisper to the screen, as if he could somehow hear me.

Shaking off my thoughts, I turn to my inbox. Lately, I've been sending out CVs left and right, hoping for anything—a new job, a fresh start. The rejections, or worse, the silence, have been rough. So, I started applying for volunteer positions too. Maybe, just maybe, something would stick. And there it is—a message from an organisation I'd applied to.

My heart skips. They work with young girls, helping them become the best versions of themselves through games and activities. I loved the idea when I first stumbled across it, but now, seeing their reply, my heart pounds in my chest. I click the email open, barely breathing.

"We would love to schedule an interview with you."

Yes! I leap from my chair, nearly knocking over the coffee cup beside me. It's not a paid job, but I don't care. It's something, a step in the right direction. The excitement bubbles up, almost overwhelming me, as I scramble to write a response. My fingers fly over the keyboard, barely able to keep up with my racing thoughts. I want to reply "right now"—to secure this chance, this opportunity to build the skills I've been dreaming of. I hit send, and for a moment, just sit there, grinning like an idiot.

My first thought is Gato. I can't wait to tell him—he's been so supportive of my new adventures. I shoot him a quick text: "Good morning! I've got amazing news!"

With the rush of excitement still pulsing through me, and a fresh surge of caffeine buzzing in my veins, I get ready for my morning walk to Primrose Hill. The dawn is just beginning to creep in as I step out of my flat, the sky a deep indigo that promises the coming day. The air is crisp, fresh, the kind that fills your lungs with life. I plug in my headphones, the soft hum of music becoming my companion, and I begin my walk.

As I move through the waking streets, the cool breeze brushes against my face, kissing my skin with every step. But my mind drifts to Gato, to the quiet worry that lingered from earlier. *Why hadn't he texted?* I shake my head, trying to shove the thoughts aside. It's too early to dwell on negativity. I push it away, letting the music pull me back into the present. The rising sun casts a soft glow over the park as I reach Primrose Hill, and suddenly, everything feels a little more connected. The universe hums around me, like wires sparking to life, sending electricity through my body.

In the distance, I spot two dogs—beautiful creatures, one black, one golden, both retrievers. They leap and bound, playing joyfully across the field. Their energy is infectious, and I find myself smiling, watching them tumble and chase one another. The golden retriever, noticing me from afar, suddenly locks eyes with me. My breath catches. He starts running towards me, and before I can fully comprehend what's happening, the black retriever follows suit. They barrel toward me, their tails wagging furiously, their eyes bright and happy.

I freeze for a moment, almost in disbelief. "Are they really running to me?" I laugh, startled, as they reach me, circling around, jumping up with excited barks, eager to play. I kneel down, their soft fur brushing against my hands as I pet them. The world melts away. Their joy, their pure, unfiltered energy fills me, wrapping me up like a warm blanket on a cold morning. It's exactly what I didn't know I needed.

I glance up and catch the owner's eye, who's walking toward us with a smile. I smile back, my heart swelling with unexpected emotion. These beautiful creatures—so full of life, of love—had chosen me in that moment, as if sensing I needed their affection.

I thank the owner as they finally wander off, the dogs playfully bounding away. As I continue my walk, tears prick my eyes, but not from sadness. Joy. Pure, overwhelming joy. It feels like the universe has sent me a message, through those dogs, through that unexpected, magical moment.

Everything is going to be fine.

The email, the dogs, the sunrise—it all reminds me to focus on what's ahead. I have an opportunity now, one that will open doors to my future, to a career helping children feel more confident, more resilient, just like I hope to be. As I walk back home, I feel it deep within me—this is just the beginning. The beginning of my new career, my purpose in life.

Chapter 35
Alone Nights, Quiet Pleas, and Silent Love

The sharp pain had faded, but the memory of it lingered as I opened my eyes. Waking up this morning felt different. Yesterday, my body had betrayed me once again—another brutal reminder of the monthly battle I fought against my own existence. It's like nature had cursed women to wage war on themselves, forcing us to endure discomfort that gnaws at our insides for days at a time. I had felt weak, both physically and emotionally, caught in that familiar cycle where my energy ebbs away, leaving only frustration and weariness behind. But today, I felt lighter.

Maybe it was because of Gato. Last night, he had sensed something, as if he could feel the weight of my pain even from miles away. Instead of the usual goodnight text, my phone buzzed with a call. His voice poured through the speaker like warmth on a cold night, and it was all I needed. Just the sound of him made everything softer, more bearable. I closed my eyes, letting his words wrap around me, pulling me into a cocoon of comfort. I fell asleep that way, with a quiet sense of gratitude, feeling lucky that someone like him existed in my world.

But sleep was fickle, and by 3.30 a.m., I was wide awake. My room was dark, save for the faint slivers of moonlight that spilled through the curtains. The world outside was still, untouched by the rush of the day, and yet my mind buzzed with a relentless hum. I tried to shut it out, to sink back into sleep, but the more I tried, the harder it became. The familiar ache of insomnia crept in, so I gave up. Fighting it felt like chasing shadows. Instead, I embraced the morning, pulling myself out of bed to begin my day.

The streets of Hampstead were quiet, dark, and drenched in a cold, misting rain. It was the kind of morning that clung to your skin, sending little shivers down your spine, but it didn't stop me. I laced up my running shoes, the chill biting at my cheeks as I stepped out into the street. London was back to its usual dreary weather, but it didn't matter. As I jogged through the sleepy streets, my headphones filled the silence with music, each beat syncing with the rhythm of my steps. The rain tapped lightly on my face, and I welcomed it, feeling each droplet as it cooled my skin, my breath fogging in the air as my body warmed with movement.

This was my ritual. The one thing that cleared my head and made me feel alive. With each stride, I could feel my body waking up, the blood pumping, muscles stretching, and dopamine kicking in, giving me the boost I desperately needed. I thought about Gato. It was Friday, and tonight I'd see him again. He'd had a long week—one that had drained him just as much as mine had drained me. We had decided on a quiet night in. No elaborate plans. Just the two of us, some homemade dinner, and the comfort of being together. I had already planned the menu: a Brazilian dinner, rich with the flavours of home—cassava soup and a fish stew simmering in a coconut milk sauce. Simple but hearty. Food that felt like love.

After my jog, I returned home, the rain still clinging to my clothes. The cold shower was bracing, the icy water sending sharp jolts through my body, shocking me fully awake. I let it wash over me, feeling every drop like tiny needles pricking my skin. It was refreshing, cleansing, the perfect prelude to the yoga class I had booked for the morning. Everything about the day felt smooth and beautiful. The movements of the yoga poses were fluid, my body bending and stretching with an ease that mirrored the peaceful energy swirling inside me. There was love in my heart—love for Gato, love for myself, love for this moment.

It's incredible how love can transform everything. It's as if the world shifts, brightens, and you see beauty in every corner, even in the smallest things. I wanted that feeling to stay with me forever.

The afternoon sunlight had broken through the clouds by the time I made my way to Hampstead Village, the air crisp but no longer biting. The fish market was bustling, vendors calling out to customers, their voices blending with the sounds of fresh produce being tossed into bags and the scent of saltwater hanging in the air. The fish lay on beds of crushed ice, their silver scales shimmering under the fluorescent lights. I found everything I needed for the evening—fresh cassava, firm white fish, and the rich, creamy coconut milk that would tie everything together. As I walked back, the people I passed seemed lighter too, their faces open, welcoming.

I noticed them in a way I hadn't before my awakening. They smiled, said hello, and I smiled back. Their warmth mirrored mine, and it amazed me how much I had changed. Once, I would have avoided eye contact, hurried past them with averted eyes and a closed-off heart. But now, I felt connected to the world around me, as if love had cracked me open, letting all the light pour in.

Back home, the afternoon was peaceful. I settled into my work, answering emails and reviewing some paperwork for the volunteer job I was about to start. Months of searching, trying to figure out my path, and finally, I felt like I was moving in the right direction. It wasn't just a job; it was something that made me feel whole, like I was giving back, using my time for something meaningful. As I worked, a sense of purpose filled me, grounding me in the present.

By late afternoon, I drifted into the kitchen, the soft light filtering through the windows as I began to prep for dinner. The chopping of vegetables, the hiss of onions hitting the pan, the fragrant aroma of garlic and coconut milk filling the air—it was a soothing rhythm. My thoughts drifted to the evening ahead, the quiet hours I'd share with Gato, and the peace of simply being together.

Everything was ready, and I still had a couple of hours before Gato would arrive. As I set the table, a soft smile touched my lips. Today had been beautiful, effortless, and I wanted to hold on to this feeling forever—the love, the contentment, the quiet joy of knowing that sometimes, the simple moments are the ones that matter the most.

When Gato called to say he'd be coming over earlier than planned, my heart fluttered. It was exactly the kind of news I needed to hear. The excitement bubbled up inside me, and I quickly set about getting ready. I wanted to look cosy and inviting, but also a little bit sexy for him. I chose a long wool skirt that clung to my hips, soft and warm, perfect for the evening chill. My top was fluffy and white, with an open back that I knew would catch his eye. Something about showing just enough skin felt like a quiet invitation, a whisper of intimacy.

I pulled my hair half up, letting the rest fall loose around my shoulders, giving me a fresh, casual look. I stood back to take one last glance in the mirror. Satisfied with what I saw, a nervous kind of thrill danced in my chest as I waited for him. The anticipation was electric.

When the doorbell finally rang, I rushed to the door, my footsteps quick and light. As soon as I opened it, there he was, standing in the soft light of the corridor, his smile as radiant as ever, his eyes—those cat-like eyes—gleaming with warmth. They always sparkled when he looked at me, as if he saw something he liked and wanted to keep. We didn't need words. In an instant, we were in each other's arms. The hug was everything—tight, consuming, like our bodies could merge into one if we held on long enough. And then, the kiss. Slow, lingering, his lips soft and sure against mine. I lost myself in that moment, in the feeling of him, of us.

That evening was going to be different. I couldn't be fully with him in the way I usually craved, my body still recovering, but it didn't matter. There was something even more intimate in this quiet, slower pace. We slipped inside, sinking into the couch, our bodies close, legs entwined, talking in low voices that faded into lazy kisses. Everything about the evening felt soft, like we were floating in our own little bubble of warmth.

Eventually, I rose to finish preparing dinner. As I moved around the kitchen, I could feel his eyes on me, watching my every move. I didn't have to look up to know he was smiling, and that thought filled me with a quiet joy. Seeing him happy made everything else fade away. I would have done anything to keep that look on his face, to hold onto the ease in his expression.

We sat down to eat, the table glowing softly under the dim light. The food was perfect—every bite rich with the flavours of home, the cassava and fish stew steaming on our plates, the herbs fragrant and fresh. Outside, the air had grown colder, but inside, the warmth of the meal, the scent of fresh bread, and the comfort of each other made everything feel cosy and safe. We took our time, savouring each bite, letting the conversation drift into comfortable silences. Afterward, I saw the way his face softened, his eyes drooping slightly. He didn't say it, but I knew—he was tired.

Without a word, we slipped into bed. Gato suggested we watch something, a documentary on mental health. It was the perfect choice, something thoughtful, quiet, the kind of thing we could lose ourselves in while we lay close. As the documentary played, I felt his body relax beside mine, the warmth of him soothing. His breathing grew deeper, slower, until I realised he had fallen asleep.

Lying there in the silence, feeling his heart beating steadily against my skin, the rhythm of it, the rise and fall of his chest, was perfect. In that moment, I didn't need anything else. Even though I love the passion between us, the heat that always draws me to him, this—this quiet, still intimacy—was what made my love for him deepen. It wasn't about the intensity of desire, but the simple, perfect comfort of being together.

Time passed like that, slow and peaceful. I didn't want the night to end, didn't want the inevitable moment to come when he'd have to leave. But I knew it would. It always did. When he stirred, waking softly, I felt it coming. He kissed me softly, a gentle goodbye, and I wanted so badly to ask him to stay. To hold him tighter, to keep him with me for the night, to wake up with him and tell him how much I love him. But I didn't. I never did. I didn't want to hear him say no.

As he got out of bed, moving silently in the soft glow of the room, he passed by me on his way to change. For a moment, he paused, leant down, and kissed my feet. It was a gesture so tender, so unexpected, that my heart swelled. I wanted to pull him back into bed with me, to let him know how deeply I cared for him, but instead, I watched as he moved away, knowing I wouldn't say a word. As always, he'd leave, and I would let him.

So, I let him go.

We said our goodbyes at the door, and as soon as it clicked shut, a wave of emptiness rushed in. The silence left behind by his absence felt heavier than before, and the questions started creeping into my mind, unwanted but persistent. *Why does he leave? Why doesn't he want to stay the night with me? What is he avoiding?* My chest tightened as the doubts tried to take hold, twisting my thoughts into knots.

I didn't want to feel this way. I wanted to push those thoughts away, but I'm only human. Sometimes the fears we try to bury surface despite our best efforts. I knew I couldn't let them consume me, but it was hard. I shook my head, trying to shake off the thoughts as I made my way back to bed. I threw on a movie, hoping it would distract me, to keep my mind from wandering into darker places.

As the screen flickered in front of me, I told myself that one day, he would stay. That the right time would come. Until then, I had to trust him, trust that the love we shared was enough. And for tonight, I would hold onto the memory of his heartbeat beneath my cheek, the quiet moments that reminded me how deeply I cared for him.

Chapter 36
The Echo of Love

It's been days since I last saw Gato, and I still hold onto the warmth of our time together at my place. He's been busier than ever, cancelling more than once at the last minute, and I can't help but feel a pang of insecurity creeping in. I never expected to spend all of our time together, but when we were seeing each other every week, it felt steady, like a rhythm we'd settled into. Now, I'm waiting more often, watching the clock, hoping for his free time.

It's almost ironic—when I prayed for a partner, I asked God for someone busy, someone who didn't have too much time on their hands. And now, here I am, second-guessing that request. For a moment, I almost regret it. But then I laugh at myself. I got exactly what I asked for. Still, part of me wonders if I should've been more specific in what I wished for. I didn't realise how much space the waiting would take up in my thoughts.

As time passes, little whispers of doubt start to surface. I try to push them down, but it's becoming harder. I'm completely in love with him, and yet, it feels like I'm standing on the sidelines, waiting to be chosen. Loving him is beautiful, but there's this underlying feeling of uncertainty, like I'm holding on tighter than he is. He never stays the night, and as much as I try to brush it off, those small things pile up, making me question us.

But then, something had shifted. The last time we met, as we talked and laughed, he had looked into my eyes and said, "We have plenty of time," as if to reassure me, as if he could sense the doubts swirling in my mind. My heart had skipped a beat, overwhelmed by his words. I hadn't responded with words—I had kissed him instead, hoping the kiss would say everything I couldn't find the courage to voice. It had been a kiss filled with hope, passion, and a quiet plea for things to stay just like that.

When he's with me, it's perfect—he's attentive, present, loving. He says all the right things, and in those moments, my heart settles. I feel secure, safe in the connection we share. But as soon as he leaves for his place, the doubts come crashing back in. It's like I'm left standing in the wake of his absence, wondering if the distance between us is growing too wide. When he's busy, he feels distant in more ways than one. I start to question everything—*does he really mean it when he says we have time?* His words say one thing, but his actions… they leave me feeling confused, torn between what he says and how he behaves.

I try to reason with myself—he's busy with work, with life. *But what about me? Do I really have a place in his world? Is there space for me in his hectic life? Or am I just a fleeting part of his day, something he squeezes in between everything else?* These thoughts gnaw at me, pulling me deeper into uncertainty. I want to believe in his words, but the more time we spend apart, the more I doubt. The more I wonder if I'm holding on to something that's slowly slipping away.

From our very first date, he told me his problem was time—he didn't have enough of it. I remember him saying it so clearly, almost like a warning. Back then, I shrugged it off, believing we'd find a way to make it work. But now, as the distance between us grows, I can't help but wonder if that was his way of telling me from the start that there would never be enough time for us.

I had always told myself I would savour every moment with him as if it were the last, maybe because deep down, I knew it might not last forever. Life is unpredictable, and love, as beautiful as it is, can sometimes be fleeting. I fell for him so deeply, so quickly, and maybe that's what love does—it transforms us into dreamers, willing to risk everything, to be vulnerable in ways we never imagined.

Chapter 37
The Weight of Words

After a long day and waking up again by 2.57 a.m., by the end of the day I was exhausted, yet I couldn't drift off without hearing from Gato. No text. No call. So I messaged him first. He replied, telling me he was on his way home after spending the weekend away. The journey had been long. I could practically hear the tiredness in his words. We agreed to talk once he got to his flat.

At exactly 8.39 p.m., the language issue was about to start, my phone buzzed. I answered, and the sound of his voice instantly made my heart melt. That voice—it never fails to fill me with warmth, like a safe place I could run to and rest in.

We spoke about our days, trading stories back and forth. I told him about the book, how I'd been sending him pieces of it for feedback. It was supposed to be a light conversation, but when we got into his thoughts on my writing, something shifted. His words… they stung, more than I'd ever imagined.

At first, I thought it was just insecurity about his appearance. *The character I'd based on him was idealised, yes, but wasn't that how love worked? Didn't we all see the people we love as more than they saw in themselves?* But as he kept talking, it became clear—this wasn't just about his appearance. He was struggling with the whole idea of being the man I'd written about.

His disbelief cut through me like knives. Each word landed sharp, cold, in my chest. I could feel the warmth from my tea fading, leaving me with a hollow ache inside. He didn't think he deserved the glowing praise I'd written for him. As he spoke, his voice held an edge of embarrassment, and his laugh, a soft, uncomfortable sound, twisted the knife deeper.

"The people who know me wouldn't believe that man is me," he said, his words rough, almost like sandpaper scraping against my heart.

I wanted to shout, to shake him, to tell him he was wrong. If only he could see himself through my eyes… then he'd know just how incredible he truly was. But instead, I was there sat alone in my bed, helpless, listening, at same time trying to convince him with words that felt so fragile, so small compared to the towering wall of disbelief he'd built around himself.

The conversation ended, but I was left reeling, my heart aching in a way that no amount of chamomile tea could soothe. His laughter still echoed in my ears, painful and distant.

I tried my best to make him understand, to convince him that he is everything I wrote and so much more. But it was like trying to catch smoke with my bare hands—futile. And then, he said the words that hurt the most, the ones that dug straight into my heart: "My friends will think is a fantasy."

Those words… they cut deeper than I could have imagined. Tears welled up, burning at the edges of my eyes, threatening to spill over. He had pierced something fragile inside me, something I had protected for so long. My emotions were in turmoil, swirling around me like a storm I couldn't control. It felt as though he had burst the balloon that held my hopes, leaving me deflated and lost, floating aimlessly in the confusion he had left behind.

We ended the conversation shortly after, with a strained "Goodnight" from both sides, as if it was the only way to stop the bleeding, the only way to retreat and regroup. When the call ended and the screen went dark, a hollow silence settled around me.

But his words wouldn't stop echoing in my mind. *Fantasy. Was that what he thought this was? Was that what we were? Or… was he right? Could he be right*? Maybe I was seeing him through the purity of my own feelings and faith—my eyes, clouded with love, elevating him into something he didn't believe he could ever be. Maybe it was me, I could had been idealising him, projecting all the things I wanted him to be onto who he really was.

The thought gnawed at me, refusing to let me rest. My mind was spinning, restless. I couldn't sleep without saying something. So I grabbed my phone and typed, the words spilling out before I could second-guess them:

"It is not a fantasy, Gato—Good night."

I sent it before I could change my mind. His reply came almost instantly.

"No, I mean to other people it might seem like that… but to us, it's real… which is magic. Night Night, Gatinha. Sleep well."

His words were sweet, yes, but they didn't soothe the ache in my chest. To me, they felt like a polite way of saying, let's not carry on this conversation. I stared at the message for a long time, feeling that familiar, sharp pang of disappointment. I didn't reply. Instead, I threw my phone down beside the bed and squeezed my eyes shut, hoping—begging—for sleep to come and take me away from the thoughts that had begun to spiral out of control.

Minutes passed, the weight of the night pressing down on me. The room felt too quiet, too still. And then—flash. My phone lit up. It was Gato, calling me.

I stared at the screen, my heart pounding in my chest. I couldn't answer. I couldn't face him, not with all the disappointment that was still so raw. I didn't want to show him how deeply his words had upset me. The phone vibrated on the mattress beside me, a persistent reminder of the conversation I wasn't ready to have. I let it ring, watching as his name disappeared when the call ended.

I couldn't do it. Not tonight. If I answered, I knew my emotions would take over, and I didn't trust myself not to say something I'd regret. I was too raw, too vulnerable, and speaking to him now might only make things worse. So I lay there, alone in the darkness, my phone silent again, wishing the night—and the thoughts racing through my mind—would finally come to an end.

Chapter 38
Swollen Eyes

As the morning creeps in, my routine is far from what I'd want it to be. It's 3 a.m., and my eyes snap open, heavy and swollen, but sleep is nowhere to be found. I drag myself out of bed, every movement feeling slow and burdensome, and head to the bathroom. As I stop in front of the mirror, I see what I've been avoiding—my reflection. Puffy, red eyes stare back at me, remnants of all the tears I shed last night. I mutter a few hollow words to my reflection, telling myself that I'm in control, that I shouldn't let this affect me. But the words sound empty, even to me. Maybe it's just my mind playing tricks, spiralling into places I don't want it to go. There's still so much left unsaid between Gato and me, so much that needs to be talked about after last night's call.

The night was rough; sleep slipped through my fingers like sand. My mind refused to quiet, cycling through the word "fantasy" over and over again, taunting me. Now, as dawn approached, I found myself exhausted, unable to escape the gnawing sadness that curled tightly in my chest. Tears brimmed at the edges of my vision, a sign of vulnerability I hadn't wanted to face.

I had cried for the first time in this new relationship, and it terrified me. The vulnerability opened old wounds, pulling memories of my toxic past to the surface. My heart urged me to embrace this love, but my mind warned me to retreat. "No more hurt," it echoed, a relentless reminder of what I had endured.

My fingers hover over the smooth surface of my Mac, trembling. The screen glows in the dark, casting a soft light over the room. A picture of Gato, smiling as if he's looking right at me, fills the background. For a moment, it feels like he understands, like he's offering a silent reassurance. I try to hold onto that comfort, but the ache remains. I know I need to write the last chapter of my book, but all I can feel is the hollow emptiness left in the wake of my words. I stare at the blinking cursor, trying to will the words to come, but all that echoes in my mind is the sound of his words.

I scroll back, re-reading the chapters I'd written about our first dates. Each word is a reminder of the joy, the laughter, and the lightness that filled those moments. Everything had felt so real, so full of promise. *How could something that felt so perfect now seem like a fantasy?* The happiness, the connection—it was all there, tangible and alive. I smile to myself, momentarily lost in those memories. There was no doubt those moments had been real, as real as the love I'd poured into those pages.

But now, with a heavy sign, I give up. The words won't come. I close the laptop, push back from the table, and decide to change into my jogging gear. Maybe a run will clear my mind, loosen the grip of everything weighing me down.

The screen of my phone glowed softly in the dim room, the missed call glaring back at me like a question I wasn't ready to answer. I hesitated, then slipped the phone into my pocket, grabbing my trainers and stepping out of the flat for my morning jog. I needed space to think, to clear my head. Primrose Hill was calling—the one place where I always found clarity.

The morning air was cool, still clinging to the last of the night's chill, but I could feel the sky beginning to lighten. The world was slowly waking up. I loved these early hours when the streets were quiet. I pulled on my headphones, letting the music drown out the restless thoughts swirling in my mind. My body moved automatically, my feet hitting the pavement in a steady rhythm, each step syncing with the beat in my ears.

As I ran, my breath visible in the crisp morning air, I felt numb. The usual rush of endorphins hadn't kicked in yet. Normally, by this point, I'd feel alive, the love and energy coursing through me. But today, doubt and insecurity weighed me down, dragging my mood into the ground. I couldn't shake it. My session with Angie, my therapist, was later that day, and I found some comfort in the thought. Sharing my thoughts with her would help sort through this tangle of emotions. It always did.

By the time I reached the top of Primrose Hill, the sky was a soft, pre-dawn grey, with just a hint of orange breaking through on the horizon. The air smelled faintly of damp earth and grass, a reminder of the night's lingering moisture. A few people sat scattered on the hill, waiting for the sunrise. I took in the sweeping view of London below, the skyline a jagged silhouette against the waking sky.

My heart started to beat faster, the familiar rush of peace creeping back into my chest.

I found a spot on the cool grass, sitting cross-legged as I began my meditation. Each breath I took felt like it was pulling me back to myself. The negative thoughts melted away with the exhale, replaced by a growing sense of calm. The quiet of the morning enveloped me—the distant sound of birds beginning to stir, the soft murmur of the city far below. My mind, once so clouded, began to clear.

Maybe part of why I received his feedback so negatively had to do with the clash of cultures and the language between us. For so long, I'd kept my emotions hidden, carefully contained. But recently, I'd opened up, allowed myself to feel and express those deep parts of me that connected to my roots. I had asked for it, yearning to be my true self, embracing my passion. Intense love is just part of who I am; I crave that connection, that vivid experience. Perhaps, to others, it might seem like a fantasy, an illusion. But for me, it's real, an essential part of what it means to love fully. I hadn't expected him to see it differently—and knowing he did leave me feeling a mix of disappointment and loss. Maybe he was overwhelmed by my intensity, or maybe he didn't understand it at all. Either way, I couldn't shake the ache of knowing he couldn't, or wouldn't, meet me there.

After a while, I pulled out my phone. The missed call was still there, but now, with the clarity of the morning, I felt more grounded. I didn't want to ignore him. I wouldn't want to be ignored in his place. But I couldn't pretend to feel something sweet or light when the truth was, I wasn't feeling like myself. I didn't want to fake it. So I typed a simple message: "I'm sorry I missed your call. I hope you get your things sorted out. x" I knew he'd notice the difference, the tone much more distant than what I usually sent. He would know something was wrong.

A while later, his reply came through. It was kind, as always, wishing me a good day. Not a "good morning"—he never said good morning. Mornings weren't his thing. And usually, I would brighten his day with a playful greeting, but not today. Today, the weight between us hung heavy, and even though I didn't want to feel low about us, it was the truth.

As I made my way back to the flat, I stopped at a small corner shop, its neon sign flickering in the early morning haze. I grabbed a carton of eggs and a bottle of water, my body craving something light yet comforting after the jog. The thought of the gym lingered in the back of my mind, but the pull wasn't as strong today. My hormones were in chaos, the dull ache of my period slowing me down, making everything feel heavier. Usually, working out gave me a release, but on days like this, it felt more like punishment than therapy.

The streets were still quiet, a soft hum of the city beginning to stir as I made my way back to the flat. As soon as I stepped inside, I flicked on the diffuser, instantly flooding the room with the sharp, refreshing scent of lemongrass. The air felt lighter, cooler. I moved through the kitchen, setting out ingredients on the counter—eggs, ripe tomatoes, an avocado, and a small tub of cottage cheese. The routine of cooking calmed my mind as I cracked the eggs into the pan, the sizzle and the warm, nice smell filling the small space. I toasted a single slice of sourdough and brewed my usual black coffee, the bitter, rich aroma blending with the citrusy notes of the lemongrass.

Sitting down at the table, I felt a flicker of peace. The sunlight filtered through the curtains in soft streaks, and for a moment, everything felt… manageable. Each bite of my breakfast grounded me a little more, the creamy avocado and tangy tomatoes a small comfort. The steaming coffee in my hand, its warmth seeping into my skin, almost made me feel ready for the day. Almost.

But then came the familiar wave of indecision. *Should I push myself to go to the gym? Or was it better to stay here, rest, and try to shake off the early morning hours that still weighed on me?* My body felt tired, like I'd been running on empty for days. I glanced at the sofa, tempted by the idea of sinking into its cushions and letting the day slip by. Maybe a little rest was what I needed.

As I scrolled absently through my phone, my eyes caught something: one of my favourite fitness classes had an opening. I hesitated for a beat before something inside me shifted. Without a second thought, I sprang from the couch, grabbed my water bottle and EarPods, and was out the door before I could change my mind. There was no time to dwell on the thoughts gnawing at me, not now. I could deal with everything else later—after the class, after I'd run myself into the ground, and maybe, after my session with Angie.

Stepping into the gym felt like a breath of fresh air, a welcome change from the chaos in my mind. The familiar beat of the music greeted me as I walked through the entrance, the steady rhythm pulsing through the air. Normally, I'd stop by the small coffee area, grab a black Americano, and spend a few moments scrolling through my phone, letting the caffeine kick in before heading to the workout. But today, I was short on time.

I headed straight to the changing room, quickly stashing my things in one of the lockers. The clatter of metal doors echoed around me, the sounds of other people getting ready to take on their own routines. I tied my trainers tight, then made my way to the gym floor, already feeling the familiar anticipation build as I geared up for the Boxing class. It was one of my favourites. The challenge, the movement, the way my body felt stronger with every session—it was exactly what I needed to distract myself.

The class started as usual. The coach, a true professional, moved through the room, correcting postures, adjusting positions, his focus on ensuring everyone's form was on point. His energy always kept the group motivated, his sharp eye catching every detail. As we flowed through the movements, something unexpected happened. Out of nowhere, Gato's face flashed in my mind, his voice, his presence. Ivan's movements, his intensity—it all reminded me of him. I found myself staring at Ivan for a few beats too long, imagining Gato in his place. My heart raced, not from the exercise, but from the sudden rush of thoughts that overwhelmed me.

Realising what I was doing, I quickly pulled myself out of it, embarrassed. *Did he notice? Had anyone else seen me drift off into my own world?* I could feel the heat rise in my cheeks. I tugged at my hair, tying it up tighter, as if that would help pull me back into the present, back to the class. I took a deep breath and forced my attention back to the exercises, willing myself to focus. I couldn't let my thoughts of Gato take over. Not here. Not now.

As the final notes of the class played out and the last of the participants headed towards the door, I lingered to help Ivan tidy up. The gym floor, once a chaotic swirl of activity, was slowly returning to its pristine state. The smell of sweat and rubber mingled with the faint hint of cleaning products, a familiar and oddly comforting scent. I chatted with familiar faces, exchanging quick, easy banter with fellow regulars.

Zack, with his quick wit and easy smile, was especially fun to talk to. We reminisced about the time I nearly dropped him during one of our partner exercises. His laughter filled the air as he recounted the incident, and the memory of that near-disaster never failed to make us both chuckle. It was moments like these that reminded me why I enjoyed these workouts so much—beyond the physical exertion, they were a chance to connect and share a laugh.

As I finished up and said my goodbyes, I felt the familiar post-workout euphoria settling in. The world outside seemed a little brighter, and the day ahead felt more manageable. But as the hours ticked away, I couldn't ignore the upcoming therapy session with Angie, and the twinge of anxiety that came with it.

Sitting in front of my laptop, the soft light from the desk lamp casting a warm glow on the room, I braced myself for the call. Angie's face appeared on the screen, her expression a blend of kindness and clinical detachment. I recounted the events with Gato—the misunderstanding, the hurt from his comment about my book. I expected some sympathy, but instead, she challenged me.

"Gatinha," she said softly, her voice filled with warmth, "you're allowing your imagination to run wild. What he said wasn't wrong; the real challenge is how your feelings and desires are clouding your judgment."

Her words were like a splash of cold water, jolting me into a clearer perspective. "Why are you feeling so insecure about him?" she asked, and her question cut through the fog of my emotions.

I tried to articulate the tangled mess of feelings that had taken root. I was frustrated that every time we spent time together, he would slip away to his place. It felt like he was leaving me behind, and I questioned whether he was truly invested in our relationship. The thought that he might be hiding me, that his promises to meet my family or train together never materialised, only deepened my anxiety. I hadn't confronted him, not wanting to seem demanding or pushy, but the uncertainty gnawed at me.

Angie's voice was calm but firm. "It's normal to feel this way, especially given your feelings for him. But remember, you can't control or predict what's in someone else's mind."

Her words offered some solace, but they also made me reflect deeply. We talked about taking things slowly and assessing how long I was willing to wait for clarity from Gato. I decided I would give it a bit more time, but I would also refocus on myself and my professional life, rather than getting lost in questions about his intentions.

By the time the session ended, I felt a renewed sense of calm. As I turned off the call, I whispered a silent prayer, asking for a sign that Gato was meant to be in my life. If he truly cared, I hoped he would reach out by the end of the day.

Chapter 39
Between Love and Letting Go

As evening settled and shadows grew long, I readied myself for bed, craving the peace that came with sleep. Just as I nestled in, my phone buzzed with a message from Gato: "Hope you had a peaceful day." His words arrived like a gentle balm to my frayed nerves, a reminder of warmth and connection. Despite the rough start to the day, his message softened the edges of my worry, helping me feel grounded once again.

We exchanged light-hearted texts, small attempts to soothe each other. I sent him something funny to reassure him that I was okay. Then, as if on cue, my phone rang, and Gato's voice filled the quiet of my room, soft and reassuring. He wanted to explain the misunderstanding from the night before, his words calm and thoughtful. As he spoke, I felt my heart begin to soften. His explanation made sense, and in that moment, I realised I'd taken his feedback too personally, letting my own excitement cloud my judgment.

By the time we ended the call, there was a new sense of understanding between us. But as I lay in the dim light of my room, something subtle but profound had shifted. The dream-like version of Gato I had built in my mind faded, replaced by a more grounded reality of who he was and who we were together.

The hours slipped by, and in the deepening silence, only the faint ticking of the clock kept me company. My tea had grown cold, leaving a bittersweet taste that mirrored my mood. I began to wonder if Gato's perception was right, if I'd been holding too tightly to a beautiful fantasy, rather than seeing things as they truly were. A dull ache spread through my chest as I confronted the possibility that our shared moments—our conversations, our laughter, the quiet intimacy—might be a cherished illusion I'd woven around us.

We had no plans to meet soon—his days were full of work and friends, and I was left with my own reflections. I found myself waiting, always waiting for a message, a sign, some proof that he wanted to see me again. He had never made me doubt his affection, but I'd become restless, craving more than what he could always give, and in that longing, I was losing touch with myself. I loved him deeply, but something within me whispered that I needed to pull back—not out of lost love, but because I have to protect myself.

I wouldn't give up on us, but I also wouldn't let my happiness hang on his every word, his every move. If Gato had doubts, if he wasn't sure I was the one, I would let him discover that on his own. I couldn't push or demand; I could only be true to myself. Breathing in the cool night air, I reminded myself that I was my own priority. It was okay to feel how I had earlier, as if my happiness depended on him—love has a way of binding us so deeply that we lose sight of our boundaries.

But I had already walked through the darkness once, and now I was determined to remain in the light. Pain and growth were intertwined, but I refused to dwell too long in those shadows. I would allow myself to feel the weight of my sadness and my uncertainties, but I would also be intentional about not staying there. Time was precious, and I wouldn't let doubts steal the joy I'd worked so hard to find. I'd rise above the fleeting insecurities and embrace the love within me, reminding myself that my happiness was ultimately mine to nurture.

I wanted to believe, with all my heart, that he was the one. He was everything—passionate, humorous, able to brighten the world just by being in it. Yet, as I lay there, a quiet but persistent question crept into my mind. "*Was I too quick to decide? Had I wanted him to be the one so badly that I convinced myself he was? Or had I, unknowingly, put too much pressure on him—expecting him to be ready for something he wasn't?*"

I closed my eyes, trying to quiet the thoughts. I trusted in God, in love, in the power of timing. But the waiting, the uncertainty, that was the hardest part. I didn't want to lose faith, but the doubts lingered, clinging to me like a shadow.

No matter what happened between us, I didn't want bitterness. Even if our paths diverged, I want to hold onto the love I have for him. He had changed my life in ways I couldn't have imagined, filling spaces I thought would remain empty. For that alone, I would always be grateful. This love wasn't a mistake; it was a gift—a gift from God meant to guide me toward healing and wholeness.

Yet, I couldn't silence the question: *Was he the one I had asked God for, or was he a guiding light, leading me toward self-discovery?* Memories of past heartbreak surfaced, reminding me of the darkness I'd already escaped. Perhaps this journey wasn't about having all the answers, but about understanding that I was enough, just as I was. The beauty of this moment was that I could love him without fear, knowing I was strong enough to find my own way if I needed to.

Whatever came next, I was ready. For now, I could love myself—and love him—with an open heart. Through him, I had learnt to truly live, to be vulnerable, to face myself with honesty. He rekindled the child in me, claiming it as part of himself. In loving him, I had unearthed parts of myself I didn't know existed, casting aside layers of doubt and insecurity that once held me captive. For this, I would forever be grateful, certain that God had placed him in my life as a gentle push from darkness to light.

Gato was a gift, a precious blessing that restored me to myself. Reflecting on all we'd shared, I could see the ways our connection had reshaped me, teaching me about love, resilience, and hope. And no matter what lay ahead, I knew I would face it with an open heart, trusting myself—along with faith, a free soul, and the deepening understanding of who I was—would guide me toward the truth.

If God is Love, through Love I saw God reflected in your eyes. In your eyes I found the force to Love Myself. God is the answer for all the questions, fears, and insecurities. Love saved me, Love saves the ones who are able to love and is denied by who cannot.

– Alma Will